31- 489

31- 489

THE ROAD.—WINTER.

PUBLISHED BY N. CURRIER, 152 NASSAU ST. NEW YORK.

MR. CURRIER
AND
MR. IVES

A Note on Their Lives and Times

BY

RUSSEL CROUSE

WITH 32 ILLUSTRATIONS IN COLOR, AND BLACK AND WHITE

GARDEN CITY PUBLISHING COMPANY, INC.

Garden City MCMXXXVI *New York*

PRINTED AT THE *Country Life Press*, GARDEN CITY, N. Y., U. S. A.

Dedicated to

NATHANIEL CURRIER and JAMES MERRITT IVES,
without whose far-sighted coöperation this book
would never have been published.

Introduction

IN THE words of that great American frontiersman Buffalo Bill, "He who brings the romance of America to Young America has not lived in vain." It is therefore gratifying to see the names of Mr. Currier and Mr. Ives as the title of a volume all their own in 1930, and to find that a great columnist and social historian has rightly decided to bestow memorial garlands, long since overdue, on two great Americans, at the same time adding a few forgotten pages to our history.

While neither Mr. Currier nor Mr. Ives belongs quite in the same niche as Mr. Lincoln and Mr. Washington, nevertheless as "Print-makers to the American People" they created a pictorial panorama of America's youth that deserves a high place in our hall of fame.

In those unsophisticated days before the camera and the movies, they succeeded in recording in colored lithographs the growth of a great Republic. There is no other such pictorial history with its record of facts, places, great open spaces, disasters and successes, achievements and failures; their pictured record of the growing pains of a nation is unique. From the landing of Columbus to the end of the Nineteenth Century they left no wall space in our history without its picture.

It is fortunate that a competent social historian has felt the urge to delve into our past while there is still the material available to fit a few of these colored lithographs that so vividly portray that past into their proper frames in our history.

HARRY T. PETERS

Contents

Illustrations

MR. CURRIER AND MR. IVES

Chapter I: Mr. Currier and Mr. Ives

HISTORIANS have always taken history too seriously. With the distressing faithfulness of unimaginative bookkeepers they have set down names and dates and places. They have seen life as a parade of wooden soldiers and they have left us the line of march.

Fortunately, however, each era has had its romanticists, too. Without them our day and age would have little understanding of things gone before. They have supplemented the gaunt and annoyingly accurate chronicles of the historians with observations born of vision less constrained. From them we have learned that men not only lived and died but also loved and hated.

Mr. Currier and Mr. Ives were, without even suspecting it, America's preëminent romanticists. They left us a pictorial record of their times inestimably more valuable as Americana than all the archives that have been gathering dust since 1492. For years they captured, in pictures as simple as parables, the charade that was going on about them. They did it without the self-consciousness of professional historians.

In the middle Nineteenth Century almost every American home had at least one of their pictures. But, for their own period, their work was so journalistic that it lacked endurance. It soon became as out of date as a day-old newspaper. Because of this fact it was almost lost to posterity. Then, at the turn of a new century, that curious creature, the collector, rediscovered the old prints in attics and in barns. Now their story has been pieced together again. It is a story the historians have missed. And it reveals Mr. Currier and Mr. Ives as more than mere "printmakers to the American people."

In the beginning there was just Mr. Currier. Mr. Ives came later. Mr. Currier was Nathaniel Currier. He was born, in 1813, in Roxbury, Mass., not too far from Boston where the process of lithographing first took root in America after a little Bavarian named Alois Senefelder had discovered, late in the Eighteenth Century, that he could draw pictures on stone and transfer them to paper.

It took some years for this new process to reach America, and it took some years, too, for Mr. Currier to grow up. By the time William and John Pendelton had established, in Boston, the first successful American lithographing firm, however, Mr. Currier was fifteen and ready for work. He found it as their first apprentice and learned so rapidly that five years later he set out for himself.

First he tried Philadelphia, without success, and then, in 1834, moved on to New York, where he took a shop at 137 Broadway with a man named Stodart. A year later the partnership was dissolved and Mr. Currier moved to 1 Wall Street, on his own. In that first year of his business independence New York was swept by fire. It was unfortunate for New York, for thirteen acres of the city's finest property went the way of all smoke. But it was fortunate for Mr. Currier.

Four days later, while the embers were still cooling, Mr. Currier offered for sale a lithograph called: "Ruins of the Merchants' Exchange N.Y. After the Destructive Conflagration of Dec.br. 16 & 17, 1835." Any metropolitan newspaper could do the

THE LIFE OF A HUNTER.

"A tight fix"

same to-day within an hour. A hundred years ago it was very different. The dazzling speed of Mr. Currier's presses was something of a sensation. Thousands of copies of the print were sold and Mr. Currier's local reputation had been established.

For several years he went on making prints of whatever he thought would interest New Yorkers. And then, on a bitter January night in 1840, the steamboat *Lexington* caught fire in Long Island Sound. More than a hundred lives were lost. Three days later Mr. Currier was ready with a picture of the burning ship, together with seven columns of detailed description of the disaster.

This time there was such a demand that he had to keep his presses running night and day. The interest, of course, was not purely local. Other cities sent for copies and Mr. Currier himself wrapped and tied the bundles and sent them away. And when those busy days came to an end Mr. Currier had a national reputation and a national clientele.

Mr. Ives came upon the scene in 1852. He was James Merritt Ives, a young man who yearned to be an artist but who was a bookkeeper because he had no particular desire to starve. He and Mr. Currier's brother had married sisters. He was first employed by Mr. Currier to keep accounts but it was soon discovered that he could do a great many other things as well. He made himself generally useful and five years later he became a partner.

Mr. Currier was tall and spare and almost fair. Mr. Ives was short and plump and dark. He was handy enough with the brush to be credited with some of the more colorful paintings which the firm transferred to stone, although there is no definite proof he did them. Mr. Currier's knowledge of art was not so practical. He did, however, pose for his artists on occasion and in "The Road—Winter," the frontispiece of

[5]

this volume, you will find him and his second wife, who was Miss Lura Ormsbee, of Vermont, out for a spin in the snow.

Whatever their contrasts, the two partners had one thing in common. Each could sense, as though by instinct, what the public wanted. They shared a keen and seldom-failing "nose for news." They were, it might be said, the tabloid-newspaper publishers of their day, seeking to catch the eye of the passing crowd with something strikingly graphic.

Theirs, of course, was a very different era. The day of sophistication had not dawned. Life was simple. Mr. Currier and Mr. Ives had only to do with the emotions that were on the surface, for no complex network had been built up around them. Man, for instance, was still primitive enough to be fascinated by danger and death —woman by sentiment. To these, primarily, they appealed.

It is psychologically true that men always have gazed with awe upon fire. Within the limits of safety they have run to it instead of from it. Early fire departments always have been composed of those who served without pay for the thrill of being near the danger. Mr. Currier and Mr. Ives capitalized this instinct. Every blaze of any consequence they reproduced in the red of cheap color to huge sales.

And it was so with every element of danger. The perils of the sea gave them opportunities. Wreck scenes were popular among those who had escaped them. When pioneers set out to conquer the West those who remained at home were eager to buy pictures which depicted others fighting every inch of the way against odds and Indians.

It is said also of early Americans that they were so fascinated by death that they inquired each morning whether there were any funerals to which they might go. They enjoyed the sense of superiority life gave them in the presence of death. Mr.

Currier and Mr. Ives, sensing this morbid interest, reproduced the deathbed scene of every person worthy of notice almost before the undertaker had called.

Sex, to be sure, was not for them, for, while it is said upon the best authority to have been existent in their day, it was not recognized. On one occasion they did print a picture of the "Three Graces," as represented by nude, and rather plump, ladies, but the storm of protest that arose closed that field forever.

However, in place of sex there was sentiment. And so they pictured the ecstasies of courtship and the joys of married life. Most of the "God Bless Our Home" mottoes were hung by the grace of Mr. Currier and Mr. Ives. Biblical scenes were turned out by the thousands. A certain Mr. Volstead is blamed by most Americans for what we call, for want of a better name, Prohibition. Mr. Currier and Mr. Ives had more, perhaps, to do with it, for their illustrations of the fate of the drunkard helped to frighten a generation into a temperance movement.

This serious background was not altogether unrelieved. Mr. Currier and Mr. Ives had humor too. They published, as an indication of this fact, great quantities of whimsical and frankly waggish pictures—social caricatures no more subtle than the slapstick, and political cartoons insidious as acid.

Through the entire panorama ran the theme of life itself, the life of a nation growing up. Ships that widened the world, railroads that broadened the nation, the first pair of long trousers, the last tooth, the beginning of woman's fight for her place in the sun, the end of the Indian's struggle to keep his place on the earth.

In what numbers these pictures flooded the nation it is difficult to tell. They were stacked in bins for sale in the shop of Mr. Currier and Mr. Ives. Peddlers hawked them through the streets with pushcarts. Agents sold them over the counter of many a country store. A firm in London distributed them over the Continent.

Collectors in the last few years have found them as far away as France and Denmark.

From the fragmentary representation that has been retrieved in the revival of interest in them a list of more than 4,000 titles has been compiled. How many of each of these titles were printed is problematical. When a print established itself as a favorite Mr. Currier and Mr. Ives made numerous stones of it and flooded the market. When a print failed to attract attention it was scrapped. It is known that one print of the "Darktown Comics" series sold 73,000 copies. Others may have done better.

The question of their artistic merit must be settled elsewhere. That some of them are hideous is not to be denied. There is a monotony about their color scheme —glaring green for grass, bull-maddening red for fire, placid blue for water—that sometimes offends the eye, for all its quaintness. There is a certain lack of anatomical proportion, too, that is annoying, particularly when it makes midgets of children.

But, on the other hand, there are many that have the touch of skill and inspiration. Capable artists were on the staff of Mr. Currier and Mr. Ives. In those days it was not at all impossible for an artist to starve to death in his garret. Few could make a living by painting alone. The field of lithography was one in which they could earn an extra penny. And so many men and women who were later to be lauded as great turned to it for bread and butter. These in addition to those who considered it a worthy field in itself.

Arthur Fitzwilliam Tait, an English artist of note, painted many of the hunting scenes, including "The Life of a Hunter—A Tight Fix." George H. Durrie was responsible for most of the New England farm scenes, including "Home to Thanksgiving." Charles Parsons made a name for himself with his marines. James E. Butterworth, with his clipper ships, Louis Maurer with his his trotting horses, Voltaire Combs with his views of New York and his sentimental subjects, Thomas Worth with his "Darktown Comics," and Thomas Nast with his political cartoons.

One artist of considerable skill did little more than prepare the backgrounds against which others sketched their ideas. She was Fanny Palmer, an English woman who might have done even greater things but for her handicaps. Among these may be mentioned a profligate husband whom she supported until one day, displaying more consideration than he had ever shown before, he fell downstairs while in his cups and broke his neck.

The shop of Mr. Currier and Mr. Ives had all the bustle of a newspaper office. The two kept in touch with events and assigned artists to cover them, when it was possible to do so, much in the way that modern city editors send out reporters and photographers.

Everyone knew that the two men could be counted on to be a step or two ahead of the times. Horace Greeley, the great editor of the day, spent much of his time in the shop, as though he expected the news to find its way to Mr. Currier and Mr. Ives before it reached his newspaper office. P. T. Barnum, who manufactured his own news as he went along, was also a frequent caller. And so was Henry Ward Beecher.

The factory that turned out the prints was on Spruce Street. There the stones were prepared and the lithographs were made. They were not, as many believe, printed in color. They came off the presses plain and then went to a great center table where a dozen women, working from a model, added the greens and reds and blues.

Mr. Currier and Mr. Ives were not the only lithographers of their day. They had rivals who did excellent work, including J. Baillie, Sarony & Major, Kellogg & Comstock, Thomas Kelly, and C. B. and E. C. Kellogg. But they endured over a greater span of years and they kept closer to their public than any of the others.

Just as Mr. Currier was the first to come, he was the first to go. He retired from the firm in 1880, with something of a ceremony, in which he presented a gift to every one of his employees. He died eight years later at his home on West Twenty-seventh Street, his son, Edward West Currier, succeeding him in the business.

Mr. Ives carried on until 1895 and was still active when he died at his home in Rye, N. Y. He left his interest to his son, Chauncey Ives. The new Mr. Currier and Mr. Ives could, of course, have kept the firm name in existence for another generation but they had not inherited the intuitive gifts of their predecessors. Young Mr. Currier, for instance, was a lawyer. And his health was such that he could not stand the strain of an exacting business. He was the first to give way, selling his interest to the young Mr. Ives.

But by this time the camera had come, and the newspapers and the magazines were filled with pictures. The fad was on its last legs. Young Mr. Ives finally sold out to Mr. Daniel W. Logan, a son of the firm's former general manager. The name of Currier & Ives continued to stand over the doorway of the shop, however, until 1907, when Mr. Logan gave up the fight, sold the stones by the pound, and wrote the last chapter.

At least he thought he had written the last chapter. For by this time the garish old prints had given way to artistic progress. They had come down from the walls of American homes and had been hidden away to gather dust. They were old-fashioned. But they were not antique. The gulf that lies between is a graveyard.

And then, just about the time they were forgotten, they were remembered.

Collectors began to accumulate them. The word spread. Hiding places were ransacked. They were brought forth again, as many as remained. The dust that had settled on them made them only more valuable.

Prices began to mount in accordance with the law of supply and demand. The smaller prints that had sold for fifteen and twenty-five cents when they were new and the folios which had brought no more than $1.50 and $3.00 began to sell for hundreds and even thousands. To-day there is a ready market for them. One—"The Life of a Hunter—A Tight Fix"—has brought $3,000.

The illustrations in this volume are from the collection of Mr. Harry T. Peters, which is one of the finest in existence. Mr. Peters was one of the pioneers in the field, starting his quest for the lost prints twenty-five years ago. He has sought them in the four corners of the globe but not with the cold, calculating eye of the collector. He has had a keen interest in the times they represent and the men who created them. He is responsible for bringing to light much of the lore of Mr. Currier and Mr. Ives.

Now no one who owns the prints would think of hiding them. Indeed, to-day hanging isn't considered too good for them.

Drawn by W.K. Hewitt.

N. Currier Lith. & Pub. 2 Spruce St. N.Y.

Awful Conflagration of the Steam Boat **LEXINGTON** In Long Island Sound on Monday Eve., Jany 13th 1840, by which melancholy occurrence, over 100 PERSONS PERISHED.

Pub. at Sun Office.

THE LEXINGTON

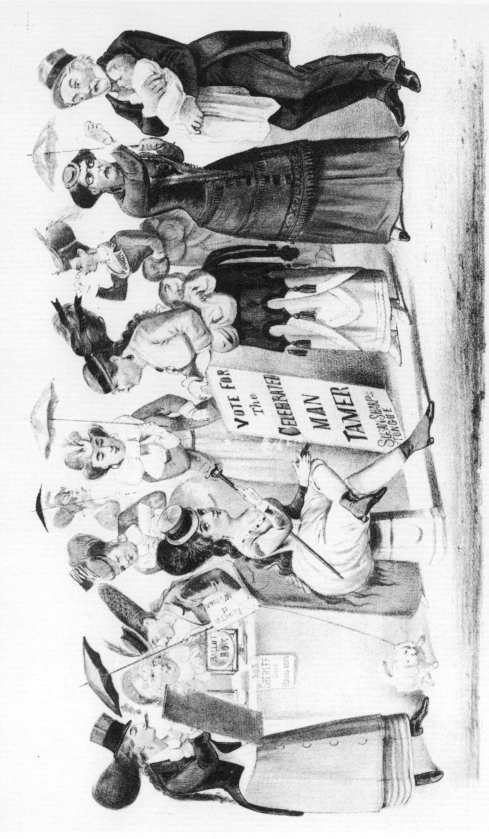

Entered according to Act of Congress, A.D. 1869, by Currier & Ives, in the Clerks Office of the District Court of the United States, for the Southern District of New York.

152 NASSAU ST NEW YORK

THE AGE OF BRASS.

or the triumphs of Womans rights

VOTES FOR WOMEN

Chapter II: Votes for Women

W HEN woman first began to doubt that her place was exclusively in the home it was in America that she proclaimed her intuitive suspicion. Mistress Margaret Brent, in 1647, demanded "place and voyce" in the legislature of Maryland. The gentlemen of that body did not even cup an ear. And that was that.

Two hundred years later woman was still nothing more than the female of the species. She had no identity of her own. She was just her father's daughter until she became her husband's wife. Her property went to her spouse upon marriage; if she earned a wage it was his. She could receive no damages for injuries. She could sign no contracts and could not even witness a legal document.

If she bore a man children she had nothing to say about them and could not even claim them on his death if he saw fit to leave them to other guardianship. She was considered depraved if she asked a divorce and, if by some legal miracle she got it, her children were awarded to her husband. If he was unable to rise from the gutter, or to leave jail, to claim them, they went to his parents.

Of course, the law granted her "protection." Man made a great deal of that fact. There was even a statute which stipulated that no husband could beat his wife with a stick that was "bigger than a man's thumb"! What more could woman ask? Well, in the next century or so, she was to think of a great many things.

In 1840 American manhood made the great mistake of permitting the inclusion of four women among the delegates to the World's Anti-Slavery Congress in London. The ladies made the long and not altogether pleasant voyage only to find that they couldn't even get into the hall. The idea that they had so much as desired to take part in the public discussion of a great question was considered immodest to say the least, and a great deal more than the least was said.

Mrs. Lucretia Mott was one of the rejected delegates and when she returned she gathered about her a group of women who were equally immodest. For eight years they brooded in each other's parlors and then, to the utter consternation of a world that was easily upset, they announced they would hold a convention in Seneca Falls, N. Y., to discuss women's rights. The general opinion was that there could be nothing about which to talk at such a gathering, inasmuch as women had no rights.

Nevertheless, the convention was held. On the appointed day more than a hundred men and women appeared at a church in which they were to meet. They found it locked. The minister who had offered them the haven had, in the meantime and at the suggestion of his elders, reread the remarks of a somewhat emphatic citizen of Tarsus. One of the women stood upon another's shoulder, opened a shutter, climbed in, and admitted the other delegates.

The result of the session was an elaborate and more or less defiant "Declaration of Sentiments," similar in form to the Declaration of Independence. It made no impossible demands. It did not even embody a request for suffrage. That was to come a few months later from a young school teacher named Susan B. Anthony and was to shock even some of the most ardent adherents of the movement who dared not hope for so revolutionary a concession.

The storm of invective that greeted the "Hen Convention" did not abate until the Nineteenth Amendment was passed and the battle was over. Adjectives were to be coined for the verbal fray before it was finished. However, at the start man was more bewildered than otherwise.

"The ladies have always had the best place and the choicest tidbits at the table," said one editor, with the conviction that the argument ended there. It didn't. The women talked back and one thing led to several others.

"The quiet duties of daughter, wife and mother," said the indignant but not altogether dignified New York *Sun*, "are not congenial to those hermaphrodite spirits who thirst to win the title of champion of one sex and victor over another."

Mr. Bennett's New York *Herald* was bitter and pointlessly facetious.

"How funny it would sound in the newspapers," it said, editorially, "that Lucy Stone, pleading a cause, took suddenly ill and perhaps gave birth to a fine bouncing boy, or that Dr. Harriot K. Hunt, while attending a gentleman patient for a fit of the gout, found it necessary to send for a doctor, there and then, to be delivered of a man or woman child—perhaps twins."

When Miss Anthony urged that women refuse to bear children for drunkards dudgeon broke its altitude record.

"She announced quite confidently that wives do not *de facto* love their husbands if they are dissipated," said one editor, who seemed more hurt than angered. "Everyday observation proves the utter falsity of this statement and if there is one characteristic of the sex which more than another elevates and ennobles it it is the persistency and intensity of woman's love for man."

[17]

As an afterthought, too, there was a good deal of resentment over the very fact that a maiden lady should even have known about such things.

Mr. Currier and Mr. Ives, in their business of reflecting public opinion, were, by their very news sense, drawn into the polemics. They, of course, were on the side with the heaviest artillery and their imaginative picturization of what might happen —but, of course, did not happen—must have set the cause of suffrage back not a few years. Perhaps they were happy enough to fear "The Age of Brass" because those who bought their pictures feared it.

But, through it all, the women held to their fight. They were refused the privilege of speaking in many cities. In others they were granted that right only to be made better targets for eggs. In one New York auditorium cayenne pepper was placed on the stove. In Albany the mayor had to sit on the platform with a pistol in his lap to prevent the use of tar and feathers.

The East was too antagonistic for early progress. The South had far too much chivalry to permit of any inroads. It was determined that its womanhood was not to be degraded by "rights." The gains that finally meant recognition came from the West. Beyond the Mississippi they knew their women weren't angels. Pioneering wasn't an angel's job. It was hard work. The women had done their share of it. They had also been responsible for all the culture and education the rough camps knew. The West respected its women and was willing to reward them for the work they had done.

Wyoming adopted suffrage as a territory in 1865 and kept it when it won statehood a quarter of a century later. Other states followed. Eventually there was a stampede. Now, of course, women have the vote and prove their right to the privilege by abusing it as flagrantly as men have done these centuries.

TEN DECADES IN A BARROOM

THE DRUNKARDS PROGRESS.

FROM THE FIRST GLASS TO THE GRAVE.

STEP 1.
A glass with a Friend.

STEP 2.
A glass to keep the cold out.

STEP 3.
A glass too much.

STEP 4.
Drunk and riotous.

STEP 5.
The summit attained.
Jolly companions.
A confirmed drunkard.

STEP 6.
Poverty and Disease.

STEP 7.
Forsaken by Friends.

STEP 8.
Desperation and crime.

STEP 9.
Death by suicide.

LITH & PUB. BY N. CURRIER.

33 SPRUCE ST. N. Y.

Chapter III: Ten Decades in a Barroom

THERE are those still alive in America who can recall a period in the nation's history when it took years, instead of just one night, for a man to drink himself to death. That day is gone. The Demon Rum has been abolished. In its stead Americans now drink hair tonic, sheep dip, coffin varnish, and other inoffensive beverages.

This situation arises from the enactment of what is, for one reason or another, called Prohibition. Because of its consummation in our time, there is a feeling among moderns that Prohibition fell upon the nation with the dew overnight. To find they are in error they need only to consult the records of earlier times. The first flask raised on these shores cast the shadow of Prohibition. It simply grew until it darkened every sawdust floor.

The date of the importation of liquor, and with it the liquor problem, is not easily fixed. It is safe to assume that it came with the first pale face. Indeed, there is a story that the very name of the Island of Manhattan, the scene of one of the first settlements, was poured from a flagon.

This yarn has to do with the arrival of Mr. Hudson. When he came ashore, it is said, he was greeted by a delegation of red-skinned Grover Whalens. For his contribution to the occasion he drew from his pocket a flask. The chairman of the committee, after a pretty little speech consisting of a number of "ughs," tossed off a healthy swig and immediately passed out. Coming to, he reported to his tribal brethren that he had enjoyed himself immensely. The rest proceeded to join him in intoxication and, in honor of the party, named the place Manahachta-Nienk, which, translated roughly, means: "The island where we all got cock-eyed." "Manhattan" was as close as the Dutch could come to the pronunciation.

Be that as it probably was not, strong drink—strong enough to be called firewater—unquestionably played an important part in the early dealings with the Indians. Beads and trinkets had their uses as currency but the traders with the most liquor got the best furs in trade for it. The French had their brandy and the British their rum. Rum was cheaper and the British usually won out because they could dispense it more liberally.

Nor was all this early liquor put to such utilitarian uses. The white man liked it, too, and was not concerned, personally, with moderation. In the early taverns, serious drinking was so common that no man was considered drunk until he had fallen under the table and was literally unable to move. There was beer and cider and rum and gin and wine. And, finally, out of the West came whisky.

A man could make a career of drinking in those days. There was always an "eye-opener" when the day began, an "11 o'clock," a "4 o'clock" and a "night cap" just before going to bed. Between times, a man's drinking was limited only by his capacity. There was no age limit. At one time children took their pennies to the tavern for drinks as they later were to take them to the corner shop for candy. A gentleman writing in the '40's tells of having been drunk before he was four years old.

Ministers were no exception. They had their rations of rum regularly. One of their number said, in 1790, that he knew forty of his fellows of the cloth who were "sots." They used every ceremony as an excuse for a good tipple. No child was christened without the guests drinking to his health, if not to their own. No wedding was celebrated without a congratulatory bowl of punch. And at funerals the mourners were consoled with something in which they really could drown their sorrow, at least for the moment.

Perhaps the deepening bowl can best be shown statistically. In 1792 the consumption of liquor was two and a half gallons per capita; in 1810 four and four-sevenths gallons; and in 1823 seven and a half gallons. In the latter year the 1900 residents of Fitchburg, Mass., consumed 100 hogsheads of rum and the good town of Salisbury, Conn., averaged twenty-nine and a half gallons a family.

It was inevitable that while this situation was developing the reform movement should develop with it. It is typical, too, that the first step in this direction should be a desire on the part of the virtuous white man to limit the Indian's supply and not his own. The Dutch were the first to include themselves in the movement, passing a law prohibiting the sale of liquor during the hours of church services. This action was brought on by roisterers who tried to outshout the good dominie.

The first temperance development with the backing of any organization came in Litchfield County, Conn., in 1782 and had little to do with moral issues. A group of forty farmers, having discovered that their harvest hands were usually too drunk to work, determined to cut off their supply of liquor. It was, plainly enough, an industrial efficiency move.

There was a good deal of hueing and crying on the subject even then. So much so that before very long the government was goaded into action. In Pennsylvania things had come to a pretty pass. Liquor had actually become currency with which grocery bills were paid. Heavy taxation was tried. The citizenry revolted—the occasion was known as the Whisky Rebellion—and there was hell, and an army, to pay.

The movement that was to sweep on to Prohibition got its start after the turn of the century preceding our own. By that time many of the nation's best gutters were frequently clogged with besotted gentlemen, and even ladies. In 1826 the American Temperance Society was formed, with branches in 222 cities. Prohibition was still almost a century away but there were enough of its advocates to enable the drive to enlist more than a million members within six years.

At its fantastic height the movement embraced every form of propaganda. There were plays, in which the plot was almost always the same: The young husband and his fondness for liquor, the temptations that led from moderate drinking to drunkenness, the suffering of the family from neglect and an occasional cuffing, the gentleman's highly gymnastic heebie-jeebies, the decision to end it all in the river, the rescue by the temperance worker, the reform, and the finale of domestic bliss.

In the field of art, if a point may be stretched, Mr. Currier and Mr. Ives did their share. Prints depicting the gaudy horror of the drunkard's fate came from their stones by the thousands, although at best they could not have been very pleasant to any but the sadistic eye. There were songs with reason, perhaps, but little rhyme, including such touching titles as: "The Rumseller's Lament," "The Saloon Must Go," "Dear Father, Drink No More," "Mother, Dry the Flowing Tear," "Are You Shingling the Rumseller's Roof?" "Papa, Be True to Me," and "Come Home, Father" with its not-since-forgotten line: "Father, dear Father, come home with me now."

In the '40s the campaign assumed militant aspects. Six young men who, ordinarily, spent their nights guzzling and gambling in a Baltimore tavern wandered into a temperance meeting and failed to return to their cups. Instead they took to the platform themselves in what was known as the Washingtonian Movement. Their meetings were magnificently staged. No man was allowed to speak, except to tell his experiences as a reformed drunkard. The confession magazines of to-day employ the same psychology. Crowds flocked in to hear the horrible details and remained to sign pledges.

Next the women of the nation discovered the cause as an emotional outlet. They had a sense of the drama, too. Their method was to proceed, in what to-day would be bridge-club formation, to a saloon, kneel in the sawdust and pray, audibly and fervently, for the redemption of the bartender and those he was serving. Many a drinker fled, never to return, and many a saloon keeper, influenced by loss of trade rather than conversion, emptied his bottles and barrels and called it a day. Carry Nation appeared on the scene a little later. She was too impatient to wait for the power of prayer to accomplish eventually what a hatchet would do immediately.

Years of such persuasion had their effect. Drinking lost its glamour for a large part of the population. Men were becoming a little ashamed of their daily nip and hid it behind the scent of clove. A moral victory might have been achieved. But, at that moment, came Prohibition. And once again drinking became smart.

MRS. O'LEARY'S FIRE

THE GREAT FIRE AT CHICAGO, OCTR. 8TH. 1871.

The Fire commenced on Sunday evening Oct 8th and continued until Tuesday Oct 10th consuming the Business portion of the City Public Buildings, Hotels Newspaper Offices Rail Road Depots and numbering over an area of Five square Miles. About 500 lives were lost and property valued at 200,000,000, of Dollars was destroyed.

PUBLISHED BY CURRIER & IVES

152 NASSAU St. NEW YORK

Chapter IV: Mrs. O'Leary's Fire

THOSE who are familiar with the bursting of bombs and the racket's red glare which have marked its latter days may find it difficult to realize that the outstanding misdemeanant in all the teeming annals of Chicago is nothing more sinister than a cow.

Gunmen may come and gangsters may go, but, in legend at least, Mrs. O'Leary's cow lives on forever—convicted without a trial of starting the fire that reduced a great city of the plains to the ashes from which it rose again.

The case against the animal is to be found in echoing song and dust-covered story. The Patrick O'Learys and the Patrick McLaughlins, who rented front rooms from them, were having a merry time of it that Sunday evening October 8, 1871. They drank milk punch until there was no more milk. Mrs. O'Leary felt it her dutv as hostess to replenish the supply.

And so, lamp in hand, she went to the barn in the rear of her West Side home, made her way to the cow and sat herself down to refill the punchbowl. It was hardly to be wondered at that the cow should resent so late and so unimportant an intrusion. The resentment took the unladylike form of kicking, the lamp upset—and Chicago burned.

That, at least, is the story that has gone round the world. A reëxamination of the facts, however, leaves room for doubt. It is true that a broken lamp was found in the ruins of the barn when Chicago's embers had cooled. But Mrs. O'Leary insisted from the start that neither she nor the cow was to blame. She admitted there had been merriment in her home on the night in question but said that she had had no part in it. The McLaughlins—Mr. McLaughlin was a bit of a fiddler—had had guests and music. But Mrs. O'Leary and her husband and their five children were in bed betimes.

Mrs. McLaughlin vindicated the animal, too. To be sure she and her Patrick had entertained. Her cousin had only newly come from Ireland and that was reason enough. But there had been no milk punch. Beer had better fitted their taste and their pocketbook and it had been obtained not from Mrs. O'Leary's cow but from the corner saloon.

The first any of the occupants of the house knew of the fire was when, at about nine-thirty, Dan Sullivan, who lived near by when he wasn't driving a dray, had knocked at the door with the news that the barn was smoking. Sullivan it was who tried to save the historic cow. But his wooden leg caught in the flooring and, being highly inflammable, was in danger of going up in the increasing smoke, and him with it, until he freed it and fled.

By that time it was too late for individual effort. The wind was blowing furiously from the southwest and it caught up the dancing sparks and tossed them to the dry pine shacks of the neighborhood. Sullivan, the McLaughlins, and the aroused O'Learys shouted as many warnings as they could and then hurried to safety.

Eventually the watchman in City Hall tower saw the flames and reported them. But he was a poor judge of distance and called a fire company almost two miles away. When the laddies arrived in the general vicinity of Mrs. O'Leary's barn the flames were far ahead of them. A wall of fire a hundred feet in height and thousands of feet in width was charging forward on a furious wind and crowds of frantic people were fleeing before it.

The city's hope lay in the sluggish river that lay between the blaze and the business section. The muddy water might have stopped the fire itself but it could not cope with the lashing gale. Shortly before midnight great sparks went sailing across the water gap, landed on dry roofs, and began a new march of destruction.

Now the entire population was on the run. Women and children led the way, the men staying behind as long as possible to see what they could salvage. There were scarlet women with the white, for the flames swept through the iniquitous "Patch" with all the fury of retribution. It was blazing bedlam for thieves looted abandoned property and fought in the red reflection of the approaching wall. Even honest draymen found that they could charge anything they desired for rescue work.

Firemen did all they could in a situation that was hopeless before they were called. The flames traveled faster than the engines and often caught them and melted them. General "Phil" Sheridan, who had saved the Union army on occasion, was powerless against so relentless an enemy as fire. He and his soldiers tried their faithful old weapon, gunpowder. But they couldn't blast a space too wide for the flames to jump.

All day Monday the city was a seething furnace. By this time Chicago had given up hope and had gathered on the side lines to watch. Finally, the blaze burned itself out. Even then the thousands who huddled along the lake banks and in Lincoln Park and even among the headstones of cheerless cemeteries had to wait hours for the heat of the embers to die down before they could creep back to the ashes that were all they possessed.

Not much of Chicago remained. Almost three and a half square miles were black ruin. More than 17,000 buildings, including stores, factories, and hotels, were gone. Almost 100,000 persons had no homes to which to go. The property damage exceeded $200,000,000.

The official total of the dead was placed at 250. That meant that 250 had been counted. The number of those who perished in the hovels and the cheap boarding houses and the dens of iniquity will never be known. Even their bones were powder by the time the grim census was taken.

Of course, Chicago rose from the ashes. Our own cities helped in the rehabilitation and those abroad sent aid, too. There are even those who say the fire was the making of the city. It was, as a matter of fact, magnificent publicity as we understand the term to-day. The world heard of Chicago because its demolition was the most dramatic story of the century. It was told in books, in sermons, in lectures, in poems, and in songs. And when Chicago began to grow again it grew to greater heights.

Even with its new heroes and its new villains, however, it has never forgotten Mrs. O'Leary's cow. But it is doubtful whether, even without political pull, a jury could be found that would convict her on the evidence.

THERE SHE BLOWS!

Chapter V: There She Blows!

IT WAS an ill wind that blew Christopher Hussey, of Nantucket, out to sea in 1712. It was, in fact, a gale. Mr. Hussey was minding his own business, which was fishing, at the time. But ill winds are known for their good deeds and when the fatigued fisherman made his way back to port a few days later he was towing the first sperm whale an American had ever caught.

Out of this incident—it was more than an incident to Mr. Hussey and those who had to listen to him talk about it—was born the most romantic American industry of the Nineteenth Century and one of the most profitable. Soon Yankee seafaring men were cruising all seven of the seas and coming home with great cargoes of oil. And every breadth of ocean deep enough to float a bluff-bowed square-rigger knew the cry of: "There she blows!"

Whaling was not new to the world nor to America when Christopher Hussey rode his gale to sea. But the sperm whale that he brought back with him, rich with fine oil, was something of an innovation. The earliest Americans had risked their red skins in shaky canoes to wound and capture the less valuable right-whale. The early colonists had learned the trick and improved upon it. But they were content to bag

[35]

only the game that came near shore. Any whale that managed to scurry back out of the sight of land was fairly safe.

Without being able to help it, Mr. Hussey had opened up a new field. Any fisherman knew that the whale was a worth-while catch. Its oil was splendid for illumination; whalebone had many uses in corsets, umbrellas, and even buggy whips; ambergris was a base for perfume. The sperm whale was even more precious, for its oil was finer and its products more numerous.

But the sperm whale kept no appointments in shallow waters. Its address was mid-ocean. So the American whaleman edged farther and farther off shore until, at the height of the great game, he was making cruises that lasted four and five years and took him to the Pacific, the Indian Ocean, and the anything but tepid waters of the Arctic.

By the time another century had set in every port in Massachusetts and on Long Island was sending its ships out in the frenzied search for blubber. Nantucket had its hey-day and so did New Bedford. Fortunes were hauled in at the end of a harpoon. Seas new to man were sailed and unapparent ports were touched. South Sea maidens and Eskimo ladies learned things from Yankee sailors that later were to distress missionaries.

Whaling was no simple fishery. It was, perhaps, the most dangerous and the most thrilling of all the industries America has known. It cost more lives than its profits could have bought.

The ships that led the chase were staunch craft, built rather for capacity than for speed, and they dared not only storms and shoals, but fields of ice. The men that manned them were hardy, heedless rovers who worked violently and played viciously.

[36]

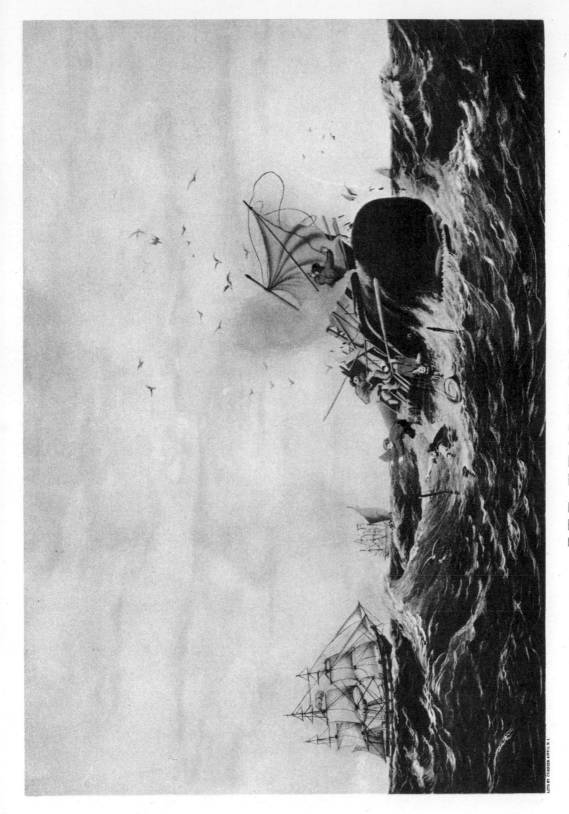

THE WHALE FISHERY.

THE SPERM WHALE "IN A FLURRY".

LITH. BY CURRIER & IVES. N.Y.

NEW YORK, PUBD BY CURRIER & IVES. 152 NASSAU ST

PUBLISHED BY CURRIER & IVES 125, NASSAU ST. NEW YORK

AMERICAN WHALERS CRUSHED IN THE ICE.

"BURNING THE WRECKS TO AVOID DANGER TO OTHER VESSELS"

PUBLISHED BY CURRIER & IVES 125 NASSAU ST. NEW YORK

THE HOME OF THE SEAL.

First there were the skipper and his mates, hard men, for the most part, so bent on discipline that they would rather crack a head than a smile. Then there were the boat steerers, men of skill and daring who handled the harpoons. The rest of those aboard were shipped for dirty work. They were from all nations. The old hands were, in large number, scum. The youngsters were boys who had been lured to sea by the promise of the chase and the profits.

So far as the chase was concerned, they seldom failed to get more than they bargained for. The whaler cruised the seas until the shout: "There she blows!" was sung out from the masthead. Whaleboats, small, graceful craft, dropped into the sea. Men bent over oars and gave their strength to the rhythmic and colorful cursing of the mate who spurred them.

Gradually they drew alongside the gigantic quarry. There was a hush and then the command: "Stand up and let him have it!" The boat steerer rose, poised the harpoon, and flung it. The next move was the whale's.

It might give the men a "Nantucket sleighride," tugging their frail boat through the water at the end of the harpoon line at terrific speed until it tired and submitted to the death blows. It might, on the other hand, sink and rise again under the boat with a great leap that sent the crew into the water in as many directions as there were men. From the moment a whale was sighted until it made its final lurch, turned its head to the sun and gave up its enormous ghost, there was adventure enough for any man.

And then came the hard work. The prey had to be towed back to the ship, which often had been left miles behind. It had to be rigged to the side of the vessel. And it had to be cut into strips of blubber and hoisted aboard. Later these strips were boiled in great pots erected on the decks. Every man on board worked night and day during this long process and if one dropped in his tracks from sheer exhaustion he was prodded back into consciousness and started off again.

So much for the chase and its aftermath. So far as profits were concerned, the whaleman did not always get what he bargained for, which was little enough to begin with. At its height the whaling industry was controlled largely by the most ruthless group of exploiters that ever sent ships to sea without black flags. There were exceptions, but they were not many.

Men were hired under a percentage system that sounded communistically fair but wasn't. Some were promised as little as $\frac{1}{200}$th of the profits of a voyage. In many cases this worked out to a credit of only $300 or $400 for a three or four years' voyage. In addition the shipowners charged the men for everything that came to their minds. Many a sailor returned from a long cruise in debt to his employers.

And there were those who did not return, too. Life in the forecastle was so vile, in some cases, and punishments for slight misdemeanors so devilish, that desertions were frequent. Some of the desertions were unintentional. There were skippers so scampish that they slipped out of port leaving men behind in order that they might steal their share of the profits when they got back home. It was in this way that the great army of South Sea beachcombers got its start.

But even if none of these things happened a whaleman's life was no buggy ride, nor would it have been so had it been all inactivity. He lived in a dingy hole and slept on a narrow bunk. His companions were usually men who kept their minds no cleaner than their quarters. His food was such as to encourage scurvy. Beans and rice and salt pork, with now and again such delicacies as duff or lobscouse or a sea-pie.

Duff was an enticing dish made of flour and lard and yeast, boiled together until hard. Lobscouse was chopped salt pork and hard bread boiled in water and liberally sprinkled with pepper. Sea-pies were heavy dumplings containing the meat, and sometimes the bones, of a porpoise caught at sea.

Few were the breaks in the monotony of the endless voyages. Occasionally there was a letter from home, left by another whaler at a far-flung port. But the news it contained was usually many months late. Now and then there was a "gam." This came when two whalers met at sea. Half the crew of one would visit half the crew of the other, the two halves trading ships.

And when he got back into port after months, if not years, of this sort of thing his was a cold-blooded welcome. The whole town turned out to meet the ship, of course, but, unless he happened to be married, there was no one in the crowd who waited for him with anything but a desire to get what money he might have.

Usually the whaleman was willing to give it up far more easily than he had earned it if he could get liquor and women in exchange. And that trade was easily arranged. Runners from the saloons and the bagnios met him as soon as he had one foot ashore, ready to conduct him to one or both and to tell him, on the way, the Nineteenth Century equivalent of the latest story about the traveling salesman and the waitress. There was plenty of time to sober up after he had been dragged aboard his ship for the next voyage.

In spite of all its drawbacks—and even the shipowners ran the risk of losing their vessels at sea and getting no oil for their money—whaling thrived for more than a century. And then it began to go upon the shoals of a changing world.

First of all came the destructive influences of the Civil War. The conflict brought inactivity and many of the ships rotted at their wharves instead of going out to sea. Many of those that did venture from shore were captured or sunk by the Confederate cruisers *Shenandoah* and *Alabama*. A fleet of forty of the craft were sent to the bottom in the harbors of Savannah and Charleston to blockade the ports.

When the war ended capital was hesitant about joining in a move for a rejuvenation of the industry. And with good reason. Oil was being found by men now, not in whales but in the ground. Wells were springing up in Pennsylvania and in Ohio, gushing illuminants and lubricants which were as good as those for which whalemen had to fight at sea.

And then the ice of the North caught the whaling industry in a death grip. The scarcity of whales had forced the remaining vessels far into the Arctic in the quest. In 1871 more than thirty ships were trapped in the ice and abandoned. Slowly the chase came to an end. To-day men still pursue whales, but not in great numbers, and the old cry of "There she blows!" is seldom heard. Not all modern sailors know what it means. In fact, during the World War, an American ship sighted a sperm whale on one of its crossings and came back to report that it had had a narrow escape from a submarine.

HORSES! HORSES! HORSES!

Chapter VI: Horses! Horses! Horses!

THOROUGHBRED horse racing has always been "the sport of kings" —at least, the outdoor sport of kings. And, inasmuch as the only kings America ever served were separated by an ocean from its race courses, the game had no little difficulty gaining popularity. Now that money is king, with a royal family numbering hundreds of thousands, it is a different story.

Trotting horses, on the other hand, have done their vying largely for commoners. Nor have they ever needed any blue blood of their own. They have always been within reach of the bourgeoisie. When America was very young, and very poor, a colt could be had for ten dollars. If, later, the animal was able to cut a fast clip on the road it meant only that the owner was able to get to town the quicker.

Everyone owned a trotting horse. Some, of course, were faster than others. If a merchant prince, out for a spin, came abreast of a butcher, delivering meat, and the road lay open for a fine stretch before them, it was only natural that they should test the speed of their respective animals. The millionaire had no advantage over the butcher in the race unless his horse happened to be faster.

The first serious attempt to race a trotting horse was not a premeditated match but the result of a casual dinner conversation in 1818. A gentleman who had drunk well made the extravagant statement that no horse could trot a mile in three minutes. A Major William Jones of Long Island disagreed. The bibber offered $1,000 as a wager. The next day the dinner guests gathered on a Long Island road. Major Jones brought forth a little rat-tailed, iron-gray animal named Boston Blue which completed the mile with seconds to spare.

The achievement was considered so phenomenal that the horse became a curiosity. It happened that Mr. Thomas Cooper, a noted tragedian of the time, was looking for something in the way of rapid transportation. He was playing New York and Philadelphia on alternate nights and found it a long trip. So he bought Boston Blue to drive back and forth.

With the discovery that ordinary horses had speed amateur racing was in vogue. Third Avenue presented a fine clear sweep from Bradshaw's in Harlem to Bull's Head Tavern on the Bowery and matches were run almost every day. Finally, in the '30s, a trotting course was established not far from Jamaica.

Within a few years trotting races were drawing larger crowds than thoroughbred racing which had been established before the Revolution. There were plenty of reasons. It took wealth to own and breed thoroughbreds, Anyone could enter his nag in a trotting race regardless of his or the horse's sire or dam.

Topgallant, one of the first trotters to achieve popularity and to win large sums, pulled a hackney coach in New York in his youth. A patron of the cabby was impressed by the speed with which he was whisked through the streets and bought the animal on the spot. He was more than repaid by the horse's victories.

Dutchman, another hero of those early days, was trampling clay in a Pennsylvania brickyard when he was bought for racing. Just what his purchaser saw in him is difficult to say for he is described as a coarse, ugly, brown hogneck, extremely un-

PEYTONA AND FASHION.

IN THEIR GREAT MATCH FOR $20,000,

OVER THE UNION COURSE L. I. MAY 13TH 1845, WON BY PEYTONA.

Time 7: 39¾ 7: 45¼

"TROTTING CRACKS" AT THE FORGE.

MOUNTAIN BOY
GREY EAGLE
LADY THORN

NEW YORK. PUBLISHED BY CURRIER & IVES 125 NASSAU STREET.

LEXINGTON.
THE GREAT MONARCH OF THE TURF AND SIRE OF RACERS.
BY BOSTON OUT OF ALICE CARNEAL.
Winner of the great 4 mile heat race against Lecompte's time 7:26 for $20,000, over the Métairie Course, New Orleans, April 2nd 1855.
Time   7 : 19¾.

IMPORTED MESSENGER.
THE GREAT FOUNTAIN HEAD - IN AMERICA - OF "THE MESSENGER BLOOD."
Foaled 1780 got by Mambrino, he by Engineer, he by Sampson, he by Blaze, he by Flying Childers, he by the famous
Darley Arabian. Messenger's Dam was by Turf, he by Matchem, he by Cade, he by the great
Godolphin Arabian; and the sire of the Dam of Messenger's Dam was also by the Godolphin Arabian.

gainly. But he evidently had the stuff for he won many races and vanquished an animal named Awful, who was suspected by his owner of having at least a drop or two of thoroughbred blood.

The trotting craze, in those early days, developed into an amazing fever. Men expected lowly work horses to do almost anything and forced them to the trial. One, for instance, a Mr. Charles Sibery, who owned a livery stable in New York, conceived the idea that his mare Mischief could do ninety miles in ten hours.

He chose a course along the post road from Jersey City to the Front Street bridge in Philadelphia and selected a sweltering day in July for the experiment. The horse was obviously in distress after the first ten miles but Mr. Sibery kept at it. With only five and three-quarters miles to go the animal broke down. She was halted for a rest. To cool her off so that she might be started again a bucket of cold water was thrown over the mare. She died.

In the years that followed there were many popular favorites, not a few of them descendants of Imported Messenger, a big thoroughbred that had been brought over from England in 1788. Andrew Jackson was so good his owners could find few matches for him. Lady Suffolk won 88 out of 138 starts. She, it is said, was the original "old gray mare" who, later, wasn't "what she used to be."

Flora Temple, a great idol, came to town with a load of cattle and was sold for $175. She beat everything in sight for many years and set the mile record at 2.24½, later lowering it to 2.19¾. Then came Dexter, the namesake of perhaps more horses than any other animal. Dexter took part in forty-nine races and won forty of them, collecting $67,000 in purses for his owners. Later came Maud S. and Crœsus and Lou Dillon, each with a new record.

Thoroughbred racing probably had its American start in Maryland and Virginia. Even before the Revolution there was a track in Suffolk County, N. Y., named for the famous Newmarket track in England. It was fashionable from the start, but there were not enough aristocrats in America in those days to make it extremely popular.

The North and South were involved in a racing rivalry as early as the beginning of the Nineteenth Century. It is unfortunate that they couldn't have settled all their differences on the track. It wasn't that they didn't try. At Union Course, Long Island, in 1823, Sir Henry, a Southern horse, met American Eclipse, of the North for the sectional title. Mr. John Randolph, the noted Southern orator, was in the stands, bestowing his finest rhetoric upon Sir Henry, but the animal evidently did not know good declamation when he heard it for he finished second.

Boston, a Virginia horse, won back the supremacy for the South a few years later and ruled the turf until Fashion, bred in New Jersey, came along. Fashion was a remarkable animal and held sway for many years, finally surrendering to Peytona in a magnificent race at the Union Course in 1845.

Ten years later one of the finest horses America has ever known came upon the scene in Lexington, a chestnut of abundant muscle. He established his superiority in 1854 by beating Lecompte in a four-mile race, in heats, to the time of 7.26. A few days later his owner raced him against time for a $10,000 bet and he shaved the mark to 7.19$\frac{3}{4}$, a record which stood for nineteen years. Once more, in what proved to be his last race, he vanquished Lecompte, with a time of 7.23$\frac{3}{4}$.

After this victory it was the plan to take him to England to try his luck against the thoroughbred cracks there. But, while he was in Kentucky resting for the trip, he was overfed just before a long gallop and went blind. It is just as well that he did not make the trip for he might have remained abroad forever and his stock would have been lost to America. His descendants have ranked among the best American horses and include the noteworthy Man o' War.

Racing received a severe blow with the coming of the Civil War. Not only were the people in no mood to patronize sporting events, but the money they had bet on the horses was needed now for taxes and for more important things. Then, too, many of the horses went to war. Cavalry officers showed a preference for speedy mounts and here were animals who had proved their swiftness. Owners were eager to help either one cause or the other and let the best of their stables go for a patriotic song.

After the war, of course, racing came back with a bound. War's aftermath is usually an orgy of gambling of one sort or another. The strain was over and men became reckless again. Wagers were large, except in the South where fortunes had been lost.

All this worked to the disadvantage of the trotting races. Men did not want to wait for four heats before they collected their money. They did not want to wait even for two, in which some of the running races were still being decided.

Bookmakers were as eager to take the easy money that was recklessly being offered as the bettors were to risk it. They arranged, for the thoroughbreds, short sprints—the sort that are popular to-day. They could crowd six or seven of these into an afternoon's racing and increase tremendously the amounts of money wagered.

And so, trotting races which could not be jockeyed in this way fell by the wayside. For many years they remained popular in the rural districts. No county fair was complete without its trots. But the larger cities, where the money was concentrated, turned to the thoroughbreds. To-day it is still called "the sport of kings." But it also attracts the man who hasn't a kingdom to offer for a horse but has as little as $2 to bet on one.

[47]

TO CALIFORN-EYE-A!

Chapter VII: To Californ-eye-a!

ON A very recent yesterday the good ship *Benjamin F. Packard* sailed into New York Harbor, anchored in Newtown Creek, perhaps the least of all waters, hauled down her flag, and lowered a ladder for the ship-breakers and the junkmen. The *Benjamin F. Packard* was the last of America's clipper ships.

Now no clipper's flash of white remains upon the ocean to remind a great industrial nation of a time when it, instead of Britain, ruled the waves. For America, over many years, was the maritime power of the world. And these same clipper ships, because they were fast enough to nose their bows in ahead of other vessels seeking cargo, were the backbone of that long-lost supremacy.

Clipper ships derived their name solely from the clip at which they traveled. The term was first applied to a group of dashing vessels built at Baltimore and sent against the enemy as privateers in the War of 1812. The British borrowed the name and the game for the opium trade on the China Coast and, so far as the game was concerned, were soon beaten at it by American shipbuilders who sent faster ships to compete. They soon controlled the trade, for the Chinese were in a hurry for their sweet dreams.

These, however, were all small vessels. The first ship of any consequence to take the classification was the *Ann McKim* of 493 tons register, a large craft for its day, built by Isaac McKim of Baltimore in 1832. It was named for his wife and built in her honor and, as frequently happens with things inspired by sentiment, was not altogether practical. Its mahogany and brass fittings may have given Mrs. McKim's pride a bit of a turn but they got in the way.

Nevertheless, the *Ann McKim* served its purpose for it proved that a large ship could be built for speed. It gave a young draughtsman in New York something to think about. And when John Griffeths had finished thinking he built the *Rainbow*— with long fine ends and a bow with concave lines. The clipper-ship era may be said to have been launched with the *Rainbow*, in 1845. On her second voyage she went out to China and back in six months and fourteen days, including the two weeks in port, loading and reloading, and was promptly pronounced the fastest ship afloat.

But it was neither a draughtsman nor yet a shipbuilder who gave the greatest impetus to the construction of these sailing vessels. It was a workman who, on January 24, 1848, came upon a nugget of gold in the raceway at Sutter's Mill, Cal. Before he himself realized the full importance of his find a mad frenzy called the gold fever had swept the East.

It seemed, at the start of that impetuous rush, that half the population had dropped everything and was bound for California. Many of them started across country. Others turned to the sea. Every sort of craft that men could keep afloat set out to round the cape. San Francisco, a lazy trading station, awoke to find itself stampeded by human cattle.

In the year before the discovery of the nugget two ships from Atlantic ports had dropped anchor in its magnificent bay. In the year and a half that followed more

E. BROWN JR. DEL.

LITH BY N. CURRIER.

DIMENSIONS:

LENGTH OF KEEL .... 208 FEET
LENGTH ON DECK .... 225 FEET
LENGTH OVERALL (FROM KNIGHT HEADS TO TAFFRAIL) 230 FEET

EXTREME BREADTH OF BEAM ...... 41 FEET
DEPTH OF HOLD .... 21¾ FEET
TONNAGE PER REGISTER 1750
BUILT BY DONALD McKAY. AT EAST BOSTON MASS 1851.

To Messrs Grinnell, Minturn & Co. This Print of their Splendid

CLIPPER SHIP "FLYING CLOUD."

is Respectfully dedicated by the Publisher

NEW YORK PUBLISHED BY N. CURRIER, 152 NASSAU STREET

CLIPPER SHIP "NIGHTINGALE":

GETTING UNDER WEIGH OFF THE BATTERY NEW YORK.

NEW YORK PUBLISHED, BY N. CURRIER 152 NASSAU STREET

CLIPPER SHIP DREADNOUGHT OFF TUSKAR LIGHT

than seven hundred vessels swept through its golden gate and left almost one hundred thousand men and women. These folk had to be fed and clothed. Ships that carried the food and clothing were paid fabulous prices for them.

It was fever, indeed, and, like all fevers, no one knew how long it would last. Men were finding fortunes in the earth but none could tell when they would dig the last of it out. Whatever was to be done had to be done quickly. Covered wagons could travel only as fast as their horses could pull them. But with ships it was a different story. And so, on the winds of frenzy, the clipper ship rode to its glory.

The first ship to reach San Francisco from New York after the great discovery was the *South Carolina*. It took thirteen months to make the trip. Before it had rounded Cape Horn on this voyage thirteen clippers were under construction. The first of these, the *Memnon*, astounded even shipping men by taking a full ten months off the *South Carolina's* time and setting a record of 120 days.

Within a year rivalry was so keen that these sleek vessels were racing around the Horn. Four of them, the *Memnon*, the *Houqua*, the *Samuel Russell*, and the *Sea Witch*, set out early in 1850. When the *Samuel Russell* put into San Francisco after 109 days at sea it was believed that the speed limit had been reached. Later the *Sea Witch* dropped anchor, 97 days from Sandy Hook!

In the ten years during which clipper ships ruled the seas for speed many records were made that steam-driven craft could not equal for years. In 1851, the *Flying Cloud* established a mark that lived as long as there were sails. She sailed from Sandy Hook to San Francisco in 89 days. Three years later she equaled the mark and nine years later the *Andrew Jackson* did the same. But no clipper ship ever made it faster.

The ships that carried men and supplies to California were more than enough to bring back what gold came East. Most of them got no cargo and so sailed on around the globe in search of it. They found it in China where the slow, bulky British East-Indiamen offered little competition.

American clippers with their lofty spars glided gracefully into Asiatic ports, took on huge cargoes of tea at high rates, and slipped smoothly out while dumpy British tubs waited. Thus they soon dominated the highly important China trade and forced Great Britain into the construction of speedsters.

Always the clippers came back to Boston or New York. The harbors of these cities were white with bellying canvas the year round. Sailing day was an event. In New York a clipper would finish loading and then drop down the East River to the Battery to take her crew aboard. Battery Park was a fashionable promenade then and hundreds would watch from shore while the ship made ready.

Swaying sailors would clamber aboard, loud with liquor, sails would be loosed, longshoremen would leap off into small boats that would take them back to shore, the ensign would be dipped, the canvas would catch the wind, and the ship would move off toward the open sea, leaving in its wake the roaring echo of a throaty chanty:

> "Then up aloft that yard must go,
>   Whisky for my Johnny.
> Oh, whisky is the life of man,
>   Whisky, Johnny.

> "I thought I heard the old man say,
>   Whisky for my Johnny,
> We're bound away this very day,
>   Whisky, Johnny.

"Oh, whisky killed my sister Sue,
　　Whisky for my Johnny.
　And whisky killed the old man, too,
　　Whisky, Johnny.

"Whisky's gone, what shall I do?
　　Whisky for my Johnny.
　Oh, whisky's gone and I'll go, too,
　　Whisky, Johnny."

The clipper ship was, perhaps, the most graceful craft the sea has ever seen. Its lines were sharp and smart. It was as solid as the fine oak that went into it. Its pine decks were scrubbed white. Its topsides were painted a black that loomed against the sea green. And towering over all were its wind-caught sails.

The greatest of the clipper shipbuilders was Donald McKay, a Scotchman who came to New York as a youth and went to work in the shipyards at $2.50 a week. He worked with John Griffeths, who designed the first real clipper, and he learned from him the new secret of speed. Upon this early formula he improved, and when he himself turned out clipper ships in Boston they were remarkable craft every one.

McKay designed each vessel built in his shipyard and followed each through to construction, watching the skeleton as it took form and making minute changes to keep its balance perfect. His ships seemed to carry his determination to sea with them. All of them were masterpieces—the *Flying Cloud*, the *Stag Hound*, the *Westward Ho*, the *Sovereign of the Seas*, the *Great Republic*, the *Lightning*, and many more.

The commanders, too, were remarkable men: "Bully" Waterman, who sailed the *Sea Witch* to the first record and later took the *Challenge* to San Francisco with a sullen crew of fifty-six blackguards only six of whom knew how to steer a ship;

"Nat" Palmer, who discovered Palmer Land in the Antarctic and who brought up many young sailors to be shipmasters; "Perk" Cressy, who took the *Flying Cloud* around the Horn on her record-breaking trip in eighty-nine days; "Phil" Dumaresq —pronounced D'Merrick—who made the trip to California in less than one hundred days on two occasions; Josiah Patten, who came down with brain fever on the *Neptune's Car* and whose nineteen-year-old wife took the ship safely into San Francisco.

The crews that manned the clippers were made up of hard but skillful men, for the most part. They were not Americans, at least not many of them. Americans gave up the rough work of the sea long before the clippers put in their graceful appearance. Yankees were too independent to be bossed and even flogged.

They were from all nations, these men who furled topsails in the worst gales the seven seas had to offer. They were Swedes and Portuguese and Italians and Frenchmen and Kanakas and Chinese. Some of them shipped because they liked it. Some of them loitered too long on the waterfront and woke up far out at sea rubbing heads that had been banged to knock them senseless long enough for them to be dragged aboard.

They were subject to strict discipline while at sea and to none when they were ashore. The pay was fair and the food, everything considered, was excellent. But the life was not easy. Almost every voyage from East to West in those frenzied days was a race, a race against time if not against another ship. It was a 15,000-mile course and one that held many dangers. The men worked night and day if there was a chance to gain a knot in the dash for gold.

When they came ashore at the end of one of these laborious voyages they were ready for anything. They were easy prey for land sharks and they needs must have

C. PARSONS, DEL.

LITH. BY N CURRIER.

CLIPPER SHIP "COMET" OF NEW YORK.

IN A HURRICANE OFF BERMUDA, ON HER VOYAGE FROM NEW YORK TO SAN FRANCISCO, OCT.ᵈ 1852.

NEW YORK, PUBLISHED BY N CURRIER, 152 NASSAU STREET.

Entered according to Act of Congress, in the year 1855 by N Currier in the Clerk's office in the District Court of the Southern District N.Y.

E. C. Gardner, COMMANDER.

their grog. American clipper ships had no liquor rations as did the British vessels of the time. Drinking had to be done ashore and few sailors missed the opportunity when it presented itself. And yet they were not a bad lot as sailors go.

At the start of the California rush the clipper ships were tremendous money-makers. They were costly to build and to operate but the thousands who wanted to get to the land of gold before it was all gone were willing to pay for the trip and the thousands who were already there were clamoring for food and clothing at any cost. Ships paid for themselves in one or two voyages.

Shipbuilders rushed their vessels through construction and sent them on their way. The trade had reached its peak in 1853 but still the ships came from the yards. Some were eventually diverted to other channels. The China trade was always profitable and the discovery of gold in Australia opened a new field. Many were used in the Atlantic traffic. In 1854 the *Red Jacket* set a record which still stands for sailing ships when it crossed from New York to Liverpool in thirteen days and one hour.

But the situation on which the clipper ship rose to its glory was artificial. Booms always fade. By 1856 shipping men began to see that they had flooded their own market. There were more ships afloat than were needed. They tried to draw in their lines. Only eight ships were added to the California fleet that year. But it was too late.

The following year financial depression descended upon the nation—a depression that lasted through the Civil War. Shipping was hard hit. San Francisco no longer demanded supplies at any price. Ships that had brought home great profits with a freight rate of $60 a ton brought home none when that rate dropped to $10. Swift clippers had no chance to show their speed. They did not even go to sea. Many of them lay in port for months at a time.

The Civil War did not, alone, destroy America's supremacy of the seas. Of course, it did nothing to sustain that supremacy. But the decline had started before Fort Sumter was fired on. It was a natural decline. The situation which had brought about the rise collapsed. American shipping interests did little to meet new conditions.

Britain, on the other hand, was ready for it. The depression might easily have had as serious an effect on her trade. But Britain had free trade and when things began to slump this proved of tremendous benefit to her shipping interests.

Britain, too, had been more open-minded to experiment. It had welcomed the use of iron as a building material for ships, whereas America had not. Within a few years iron had won its place upon the seas and the British were far ahead of all other nations in tonnage of this sort. It was a simple matter to corner the trade of the world.

By the time economic conditions had righted themselves clipper ships were outmoded. Iron ships studded the seas and steam was the power that was driving them, not wind.

The old clippers gradually disappeared. Some rotted away in port. Some sank at sea when they tried rounding the Horn as they had done in their youth. Some burned to the water's edge. And some, the *Benjamin F. Packard*, for example, just anchored and lowered their ladders and let the shipbreakers and the junkmen climb aboard and claim them.

MRS. BLOOMER'S MILLERS

Chapter VIII: Mrs. Bloomer's Millers

EVEN Time has a way of misbestowing its memorial garlands now and again, and so it is that the name of Mrs. Amelia Jenks Bloomer endures fallaciously in the vocabulary of a nation that has forgotten her long since.

In the bloomers of the modern feminine wardrobe the lady has her slightly misplaced nimbus. But the etymology is, to say the least, inexact. Mrs. Bloomer did not devise the garment that, by various developments, has brought her memory at this late date to the lingerie counter. Nor was she even the first to wear it. Bloomers, rightly named, would be millers. But it is a little too late to do anything about that.

Amelia Jenks, the daughter of an upstate New York clothier, became Mrs. Bloomer in 1830 by the fairly simple process of marriage to Dexter C. Bloomer, a Quaker newspaper publisher of Seneca Falls, N. Y. Mr. Bloomer evidently was not of the emotional type, for he reveals in his memoirs that what he discerned chiefly in his lady's love letters during their courtship was an ability to write for the newspapers and magazines.

When they had settled down in Seneca Falls he urged her to capitalize this gift.

Mrs. Bloomer, however, needed inspiration. She found it soon afterward, it seems, in the Washingtonian Temperance Reformation, a feverish movement of the '40s, started by six gentlemen of Baltimore who had been efficient drunkards most of their lives but who had sobered up one fine morning to a point of high militancy against the Demon Rum. Two of them visited Seneca Falls to denounce their old bottled friend and left Mrs. Bloomer in such a state of excitement that she sat right down and wrote a series of articles for the *Water Bucket*, a temperance publication.

It was not long afterward that she became interested in the activities of a small but earnest feminine group bold enough to believe that women had a few rights of their own in this world and determined enough to claim them. Mrs. Elizabeth Cady Stanton, also of Seneca Falls, was one of these and probably helped call Mrs. Bloomer's attention to the shackled state of her sex.

The fine, forceful literary style that Mr. Bloomer had discovered in his courtship mail was thus thrown into the battle for women's rights. In 1849, the better to wage the fight, Mrs. Bloomer started a journal of her own, probably the first in this country to be published by a woman. It was called *The Lily*, although Oscar Wilde could not have had anything to do with that, not having been born until seven years later.

It isn't of record that Mrs. Bloomer gave a great deal of thought to the question of women's emancipation from dust-sweeping skirts until 1851. In that year Mrs. Elizabeth Smith Miller, a daughter of Congressman Gerrit Smith of New York, visited her cousin, Mrs. Stanton, in Seneca Falls. Three or four months before, Mrs. Miller had startled Washington by appearing "dressed somewhat in Turkish style." Above the waist her costume complied with all the conventions of the Western Hemisphere. Below, however, she wore a skirt which extended barely beyond the knee, underneath which were full, baggy trousers of broadcloth, gathered together at the ankle with an elastic band. In this garb she strode into Seneca Falls.

The conveniences of the new costume were obvious. Mrs. Bloomer adopted it at once as another step toward freedom. So, for that matter, did Mrs. Stanton, Lucy Stone, Susan B. Anthony, Dr. Harriet M. Austin, Paulina Wright Davis, Celia Burleigh, and all the leaders in the movement that was to result many years later in a Nineteenth Amendment to the Constitution. Mrs. Bloomer did no more than follow with the rest.

But Mrs. Bloomer had *The Lily* at her command and through its columns immediately launched upon a campaign of reform in women's dress based on the new costume. The circulation leaped by thousands and carried the lady's name to all corners of the land. The daily press took it up, quoting from her journal. It was only a matter of months until she was identified inseparably and forever with the garment. The movement became known as Bloomerism, its followers as Bloomerites, and the trousers as bloomers.

It is, perhaps, unnecessary to say that the fight was never won. Those who wore the garb of freedom attracted only curious stares at the start. Then there were jeers. Hoodlums went to all the trouble of learning a song with which to mock. Its lyric ran:

> "Heigh ho! in rain and snow,
> The bloomer now is all the go!
> Twenty tailors take the stitches!
> Twenty women wear the breeches!
> Heigh ho! in rain and snow,
> The bloomer now is all the go!"

It sounds rather inane now and it couldn't have sounded much better then, but it hardly seems worth fighting over at any time. However, the bloomer girls of the

'50s found that their male escorts were frequently moved to such indignation that they threatened to cane the serenaders. It all became very embarrassing.

The weaker sisters, unable to stand the gaff of ridicule, dropped by the wayside quickly, returning to the slavery of long skirts. Even the sturdier ones found excuses to abandon the trousers within a few years. Mrs. Stanton said that her dear old father objected to the costume. Lucy Stone announced that the dignity of advancing years demanded a return to the conventions. It did not, however, demand that she assume her husband's name.

Mrs. Bloomer was perhaps the last to give up. She held on for eight years, probably because she knew she was identified more than the others with the garment and that wearing it was expected of her. Her husband moved to Iowa and she went along with him. The change gave her an opportunity to make the break and soon after her arrival there she wrote to a friend that the high winds of the West "played sad work with short skirts" so she had gone back to long ones. The trousers went, too.

The developments which brought the garment to its present state are not clear. Now, of course, it is shorter and filmier and runs to the pastel shades. But it keeps Mrs. Bloomer's name. It seems a little curious that with the lady herself gone and forgotten almost any gust of wind can lift a feminine skirt and reveal the only monument she has in a day and age when both prohibition and women's suffrage, her favorite causes are written into the Constitution.

THE BLOOMER COSTUME.

FIREMAN, SAVE MY CHILD!

Chapter IX: Fireman, Save My Child!

THE original inhabitants of the island of Manhattan were not greatly concerned with fighting fire. It was created by the somewhat trying process of rubbing two sticks together and the Indian did not go to all that trouble unnecessarily. If it got beyond control he simply walked away from it, taking his portable residence with him.

It was the pale face, as he was not so laughingly called in those days, who brought complications. Dutch settlers were less rugged and demanded shelter that was more substantial and less mobile. They built their houses with the material at hand, using wood even for their chimneys, and adding thatched roofs that were highly inflammable.

Naturally it was only a question of time until fire fighting became a community problem. Prevention evidently did not immediately occur to the villagers. There was plenty of water, the island being surrounded by it, and they evidently were content to carry it in crude buckets and dash it on their burning domiciles when the occasion demanded.

The peg-legged Mr. Stuyvesant, when he took charge of the colony in 1647, realized that steps had to be taken. He began by placing a ban on wooden chimneys.

He also appointed four Worshipful Fire Wardens to enforce his law and to inspect all hearths. Fires diminished for a time, but as the years passed the Wardens became decreasingly worshipful in the eyes of the *goede vrouws*, who found their inspection visits bothersome and treated them to such thorough-going abuse that the office soon went begging and sparks fell where they pleased.

The situation needed a calamity to rouse the burghers to self-protection and it came on a bitter night in 1657 when a log rolled out of the fireplace in the home of Samuel Baxter and set it blazing. Buckets were scarce and, by the time the few that could be found had been filled, the finest mansion on the island was in ashes.

The loss was a blow to civic pride and now the Council lost no time in dealing with the problem. Each household was taxed one beaver or eight guilders in sewant, a currency made from shells, for the purpose of providing hooks and ladders and 250 leather buckets. The town's cobblers were prevailed upon to make the buckets and a year later they were completed and distributed—fifty in the City Hall, fifty in Daniel Litchoe's tavern, and others in the homes of prominent burghers.

Not long after, too, a rattle-watch was created, each burgher serving his time patrolling the town at night, keeping an eye out for the skulking culprit and also for the curling smoke that warned of fire. When the latter was sighted hideous rattles woke the town and all turned out to fight the flames.

When the English came in the name of the Duke of York they brought system with them. Bucket ownership was made compulsory for each householder. It was decreed, also, that when the rattle sounded each citizen should open his window and toss out his bucket. Members of the guard gathered them up and hurried to the blaze. Then all available men—and women, too—followed them and formed two

THE LIFE OF A FIREMAN.

The Metropolitan System.

NEW YORK, PUBLISHED BY CURRIER & IVES, 152 NASSAU ST.

lines between the fire and the nearest well or pump. One line handed on the water-filled buckets, the other passed back the empties. It wasn't much fun.

In 1731, Richard Newsham, an Englishman, invented a fire engine. It was a cumbersome affair into which water was poured, then pumped by hand through a pipe to spurt a feeble stream. But it was an improvement and the aldermen of New York bought two of them immediately and installed them in sheds behind the City Hall. That they were not altogether efficient is indicated by a newspaper account of a blaze in a joyner's house a few days later. It is recorded that "by the aid of the two fire engines which came from London in the ship *Beaver* the fire was extinguished after having burned down the house and damaged the next."

However, the two engines served to bring about the formation of a real fire department, commanded first by Anthony Lamb and later by old Jacob Turk, who devised the leather helmets which still are worn. This early fire corps developed within a few years into a volunteer department which was to serve the city for more than a century and a quarter.

The story of the volunteers is an amazing chronicle. The organization was born of civic pride and into it crowded the fathers and sons of the best families of the day. They received no pay, but membership was considered an honor. Companies popped up all over the city. When the fire bell sounded merchant princes and wealthy scions dropped whatever was at hand, rushed to their firehouses, donned their leather hats, dragged their pet engines through the streets, and proceeded to risk their lives.

Fire companies became social organizations of high standing. They gave balls and chowder parties. Engines became objects of endearment, known fondly by such names as "Old Wreath of Roses," "Lady Washington," and "Red Rover," and were even embraced and kissed in public when they had performed valiantly. Com-

[69]

panies raced each other to fires and were intense rivals in the matter of efficiency. All this, at the beginning, was so much fire insurance.

As time wore on, however, the rivalries became less than friendly. Feuds developed and became more important than the job at hand. At the sound of an alarm one company would send out advance runners to cover the nearest water hydrant with a barrel so that it could not be found by earlier arrivals. Hostile corps, meeting on the way to a blaze, might be expected to plunge into their personal warfare with fists. Unfortunately, the flames did not wait for the decision.

Things went from bad to much worse. Brawlers and gangsters were recruited for their ability to fight men rather than fire. The volunteers became politically influential and belligerently independent and stubborn. Horses were introduced to draw engines in London but for years they were spurned in New York because the volunteers enjoyed dragging their engines themselves. Steam engines were invented but the volunteers would not permit their dilapidated old pets to be replaced by them.

Eventually civic pride again took a hand, and in 1865 the State Legislature was induced to create for the city the Metropolitan Fire Department, an organization of paid firemen. The volunteers threatened to hold their firehouses against all comers but in the end they capitulated and the newcomers went to work in their bright red shirts. Since then the situation has been under control.

EROS GO BRAGH!

Chapter X: Eros Go Bragh!

SEX, we are told, raised its ugly head in the Garden of Eden, looked about without abashment for an eon or two, and then, for no important reason that can be discovered, buried it in the sand on a June dawn in 1837 when a very young lady was called from her too, too virtuous couch to become the Queen of England.

It is typical of Victoria that she felt it necessary to slip on a dressing gown before she could hear the news. Of course, it was her privilege to be a good queen, as she promised that daybreak. But Victoria abused the privilege. It took the world—the English-speaking world, at least—a great many years to rediscover what was underneath the dressing gown.

During those years the world was almost complex in its simplicity. The effort it made to deny reality was worthy of a better cause. It began by making woman an angel. It may have been a good idea at the time, but in years to come it was to prove something of a handicap even for women. Angels, it turned out, were supposed to stay in heaven, as represented by the home.

However, for the era which took its name from the good Queen, it worked out ridiculously well. The ladies—it was almost impossible to mention them without invoking God's blessing upon them—were overwhelmed with what the male of the species proudly regarded as protection. It was entirely too easy. Whenever they were confronted with any situation which, for one reason or another, they desired to evade they had only to faint and turn up their pretty toes.

Toes, too, were all they could turn up. Man—that is, the gentleman—had no legitimate reason even to suspect that woman had legs. Never, under any circumstances, could she hint that she had them. She had a waist—that much could be seen. She had feet. Men who were unworthy of the name sometimes peeked as ladies were descending staircases and made the discovery that she had ankles. The rest was mystery.

There were, occasionally, references to indefinite anatomical objects which were known as limbs. But no one with any breeding was expected to know what was meant by these references.

There is for instance the story of the young lady who was injured in a railway accident. A doctor found her pinned down by the débris and evidently in pain that might well have broken down the barriers even of good taste.

"Where are you hurt?" he asked.

"One of my limbs is broken," she replied, as demurely as she could under the circumstances.

The doctor, of course, made an effort to find out which of her limbs was fractured. He reckoned without the influence of the good Queen of England. The young lady would not answer a direct question. But finally, by a great stroke of diplomacy, he managed to meet the situation.

"Is it," he asked, blushing into his beard, "the limb with which you thread a needle?"

[74]

"No," she replied, turning her head, "it is the limb on which I wear a garter."

The mere suspicion that a lady was immodest in this matter of legs was enough to stamp her as one fallen from grace. A matron in New England was sued at law by another for no greater offense than remarking in mixed company that she believed the other had lifted her skirts a little too high in crossing the street on a rainy day. An actress in New York achieved the reputation of one who "dared do anything" because of a pert habit of standing on one foot and kicking up her dresses behind.

Indeed, so sure were the ladies of America that their precious legs would never be seen that they did not care how they looked. If any proof of this is needed there are statistics to show that at the turn of our own century only one pair of silk stockings was sold annually for every two thousand inhabitants of these United States.

The young lady was brought up to be very wary of the young man. Among the taboos of the era, found in an etiquette book, were these:

"Sitting cross-kneed; sitting too closely; permitting a man to inspect a bracelet or a brooch without removing the object to be inspected; reading with a gentleman off the same book or newspaper; suffering a gentleman to touch your curls; humming a tune before a strange gentleman; slapping a gentleman with your fan even in fun."

Not only did all this quaint modesty apply to the human form. Its representation in art was subject to the same curious censorship. Victoria herself refused to permit an artist to adorn her garden house with nudes. Evidently she could not trust herself not to swoon at the sight of them. The attitude was reflected in America in a more pronounced way. If individuals or galleries brought themselves to buy a replica of a lady in the altogether because of its artistic reputation it was immediately draped with petticoats that its own marble modesty might be preserved.

The angelic qualities of women were guarded in other ways, as well. A man who

[75]

would smoke in the presence of a lady was considered nothing short of depraved. In fact, so sensitive was she considered even to the aroma of tobacco that men who indulged in cigars and cigarettes ate parsley to kill the scent before joining the ladies.

Swearing within feminine hearing was an offense. Viscount Melbourne, who was Victoria's first prime minister, had a difficult time suppressing his favorite word, which was "Damn!"—but he accomplished it. Eventually it became extremely bad form to forget oneself to the extent of "the dickens!" or even "Goodness!"

But while sex was thus being abased, love was being exalted. They were, of course, separate and distinct, one having no relation whatever to the other. If there be any doubt on this point it is dispelled by records of the naïve custom known as bundling. For the sake of authenticity, it must be admitted that this curious practice obtained a day before Victoria's but the principle involved remained alive throughout the age of innocence.

Bundling was a custom of staid New England. In a time when it was considered immoral for a young couple to hold hands it made its appearance. In those days houses were far apart. A swain often found himself at his young lady's home, cut off from his own by distance or a storm. Houses were small and accommodations were few. So nothing was considered more natural than that the two should sleep together —each fully clothed, of course. It was all very chaste. Or, at least, if it wasn't there was a hasty wedding.

Bundling was no more than an innocent incident in courtship, which, then and in the days that were to follow before a younger generation turned rebel, was an elaborate and formal affair. The holy state of matrimony was approached with all the pretentiousness that complex sentiment could build up.

First there were the long evenings in which a man and a maid could talk of

KISS ME QUICK.

Children: this is the third time within an hour that I have placed your hats properly upon your heads.— There!!

THE LOVERS QUARREL.

THE LOVERS RECONCILIATION.

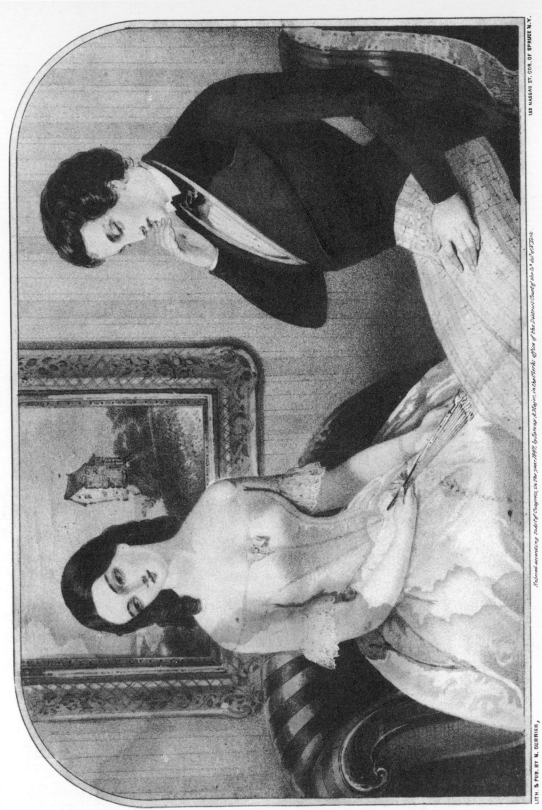

LITH. & PUB. BY N. CURRIER,

POPPING THE QUESTION.

506.

152 NASSAU ST. COR. OF SPRUCE N.Y.

Entered according to act of Congress, in the year 1846, by Currier & Major, in the Clerk's office of the District Court of the S. Dist. of N. York.

Entered according to Act of Congress in the year 1847 by N. Currier, in the Clerks office of the District Court of the Southern Dist. of N.Y.

392.

MARRIED.

Entered according to Act of Congress in the year 1847 by Currier & Magee, in the Clerks office of the District Court of the Southern Dist. of N.Y.

391.

SINGLE.

everything but love. They were not so long as they seemed, as a matter of fact, for a swain could never stay beyond nine o'clock. On these occasions there was a good deal of boasting and there was also a good deal of giggling.

It would seem from a consultation with contemporary literature that no man ever asked a maid to marry him. It was not that direct. Instead he "popped the question." This, of course, was never done without interminable preliminaries. If he was every inch a gentleman he first conferred with the father of the young lady and asked that worthy gentleman whether he had any objections to the opening of negotiations.

Once this was done, the "question" was "popped." Regardless of whether the young man had been wearing out the red plush of the parlor for years, it always came as a surprise. And it never met with a definite answer. It was always referred back to Father.

Often the approach was less direct. The bashful beau could not nerve himself to the point of "popping." In this case he merely assumed, after a year or two of what was known as "keeping company," that he had been elected. Eventually he steeled himself to ask whether the lady was not, perhaps, "ready to name the happy day." She was surprised, of course, and referred him to Papa. There was no escaping that male parent, unless he happened to be in his grave. In that case it was Mama who made the decision. And if Mama had joined the saints, as the saying was, there was bound to be a guardian.

Even after the ultimate result of the courtship was decided there was no "necking." A chaste kiss sealed the pact and perhaps one or two were stolen later, but the commentators on good manners warned:

"Hugging and kissing are all very well when not indulged in too often."

The fiancé found his chief enjoyment in writing impassioned letters to his love. At least, he considered them impassioned. Etiquette books of the period gave samples of those considered proper. For example:

"My Dearest Amelia:

"I cannot refrain from writing you a few lines to-day, although we parted so recently. My thoughts are constantly with you and your pleasant face and sweet smile seem even now before my mind's eye.

"I do not know that it is much satisfaction to you to be so reminded of my love and devotion but it is a pleasure to me to speak my thoughts on the subject. Be that as it may, I am sure my whole soul is with you and the only anxiety I have is the fear that I may not be enabled to prove myself worthy of your generous confidence. I shall do my best, however, to merit your constant love, waiting and hoping for the day when we part no more.

"[Here you can put in your own talk or gossip.]

"With further assurance of my entire devotion, I remain as ever, my dear girl, your affectionate friend and lover."

Or this, for one who was determined to "pile on the agony," as the phrase of the day had it:

"My Bonnie Kate:

"Some philosopher has remarked that when a man is once thoroughly in love it changes the whole scope of his thoughts, feelings, ideas—that he, in short, is not the same individual in point of intellect that he was before he experienced the delightful sense of a sincere personal attachment. This seems to me a rational theory.

"When I reflect upon my position as your favored friend my happiness knows no bounds. The sun of heaven shines bright and glorious. I never felt so before. Success in business matters may have been cheering but yet my happiness was incomplete. I lacked a loving heart to beat in unison with my own.

"In your affection, my dearest Kate, I have found consolation, and I hope and trust that our future career will be one of happiness unalloyed. I hope always to merit your unaffected regard.

"[Here put in the information you desire to communicate.]

"Hoping that our mutual sympathy may continue while life lasts, I remain, Katy darling, your faithful friend and affectionate lover."

To a modern Katy darling it would be cause enough for the breaking of an engagement. The Katy of the Victorian Era cherished it and kept it with others in the same handwriting, all tied together with a dainty blue ribbon.

Of course she did not have to remain engaged if she did not want to. It was her privilege to break the relationship and hers only. A man might know that he was making, in matrimony, the greatest mistake of his life and one that might easily wreck it, but he was expected to die rather than ask to be released from the promise he had asked.

They might quarrel, too, and frequently did. In which case it was always the man who was in error. An angel could not be wrong. He did the apologizing in every case and the lady did the accepting, after the proper display of pouting.

Nor did she take the first man who came along, necessarily. Of course there were cases in which the eager father, realizing he had something of a frump on his hands, waited in the upstairs shadows during the courtship and as soon as he heard the proposal rushed out with upraised hands and a more than generous "Bless you, my children!"

There were plenty of rules to guide the girl, as well as the man, in a selection of a mate. Perhaps modern physicians, and, more probably, modern psychiatrists, would not give them their approval, but men of science were no more consulted in those days than they are now.

Etiquette books frequently gave gratuitous advice on the subject. For instance:

"Bright red hair should marry jet black, and jet black, auburn, or bright red, etc. And the more red-faced and bearded or impulsive a man, the more dark, calm, cool, and quiet should his wife be. The florid should not marry the florid, but those who are dark in proportion as they themselves are light.

"Red-whiskered men should marry brunettes, but not blondes; the color of the whiskers being more determinate of the temperament than that of the hair.

"The color of the eyes is more important. Gray eyes must marry some other color, almost any other, except gray; and so of blue, dark, hazel, etc.

"Those who have little hair or beard should marry those whose hair is abundant; still, those who once had plenty, but have lost it, may marry those who are either bald or have but little; for in this, as in other cases, all depends on what one is by nature, little on present states.

"Men who love to command must be especially careful not to marry imperious, women's-rights women; while those who willingly 'obey orders' need just such.

"A timid woman should never marry a hesitating man, lest, like frightened children, each keep perpetually re-alarming the other by imaginary fears; nor yet a careless man, for he would commit just indiscretions enough to keep her in perpetual fear and trembling; but should marry one who is bold, yet judicious, so that her intellect, by reposing in his tried judgment, can feel safe, and let her trust in him quiet her natural fearfulness.

"Men large in beauty should by no means marry women deficient in it: yet women in whom it is large may marry men in whom it is only fair, provided other traits are favorable; for a man of taste can never endure a slattern, while a woman of taste can bear with a man who is careless of appearances, and love him, provided he has sufficient power and stamina of character to eclipse this defect by his sterling characteristics; yet he must let her 'fix him up nicely.'"

As for marriages, they were always happy. That at least was the story to which the age of innocence stuck until a day when divorce was not considered altogether disgraceful. It was a strange era—with virtue blind, and deaf to everything but sentiment.

Heigh ho, as Mr. Noel Coward so recently and so lyrically and so aptly has remarked, if love were all!

MY HAT AND FISTICUFFS!

PUBLISHED BY CURRIER & IVES.

152 NASSAU ST NEW YORK.

TOM SAYERS CHAMPION OF ENGLAND.

Born at Pimlico, Brighton, Sussex 1826.

HEIGHT 5 FEET 8 INCHES. LOWEST FIGHTING WEIGHT 10 ST 10 LBS

Beat Abt Couch. March 19, 1849, £ 5 a side.
Beat Dan Collins, April 20, 1851, £ 25 a side.
Beat Jack Grant, Nov. 29, 1852, £ 100 a side.
Beat Jack Martin, Jan. 26, 1853, £ 100 a side.
Beaten by Nat Langham, Oct. 18, 1853, £ 100 a side.
Beat George Sims, Feb. 2, 1854, £ 50 a side.
Beat Harry Poulson, Jan. 29, 1856, £ 50 a side.

Beat Aaron Jones, Feb. 19, 1857, £ 100 a side.
Beat Tipton Slasher, June 16, 1857, £ 200 a side.
Beat Bill Benjamin, Jan. 5, 1858, £ 200 a side.
Beat Tom Paddock, June 15, 1858, £ 100 a side.
Beat Bob Brettle, Sep. 5, 1858, £ 200 a side.
Beat Bob Brettle, No. 20, 1859, £ 200 a side.
Fought J. C. Heenan, 42 Rounds and drawn Apr. 17, 1860.

JOHN MORRISSEY.

Born February 5th, 1831.

HEIGHT 6 FEET, WEIGHT 170 LB*

Beat Thompson, Aug. 31, 1852, 11 Rounds 10 min.
$ 2000 a side. — California.
Beat Yankee Sullivan, Oct. 12, 1853, 37 Rounds 55 min.
$ 2000 a side. — Boston Corners, N.Y.

Beat John C. Heenan, "The Benicia Boy" Oct. 20.
1858, 11 Rounds, 28 min. $ 2500 a side.
Long Point Canada.

Chapter XI: My Hat and Fisticuffs!

THE figure of John Morrissey cast a hulking shadow upon the American scene in that curious era characterized by both bare knuckles and white gloves. The one symbolized a waning rowdyism; the other a dawning elegance. Morrissey's fists were bare at the start and he scarred them on the heads of men in achieving fame. But he lived to draw white gloves over their ugliness.

Morrissey was born in Ireland in 1831, and bobbed up ten or twelve years later in Troy, N. Y., a long way from his native Tipperary. On that occasion his father had to take him out of school. The lad, it seems, was so fond of fighting that he threatened to depopulate the classroom by thrashing every boy who could not run faster than he.

For a time his prodigious strength was turned into less devastating channels. He became a river deckhand. His real ambitions, however, were gladiatorial, rather than industrial and when his business took him to New York he hunted out the rendezvous of convivial cut-throats, a saloon conducted by Captain Isaiah Rynders. Through the smoke of this barroom he strode until he had reached the center. Then he folded his arms across his great chest and announced:

"I can lick any man in the place."

The assembled thugs accepted his challenge enthusiastically—and collectively. They pounced upon him with bottles, pitchers, and chairs. In the end they even sacrificed a fine old earthenware cuspidor. When this was brought down on his head Morrissey became quite calm and remained so for almost twenty-four hours in spite of all the doctor could do. Then he went back to Troy to mend.

The début was not a total failure. Morrissey had fought until senseless, and gameness was a quality admired by Captain Rynders. When the young gladiator returned to the city, which he did as soon as the bandages were removed, the captain found work for him as an emigrant runner. These gentlemen welcomed newcomers to the land of the free and guided them to spots where they could be either mulcted or brought up to vote the proper ticket.

There was intense rivalry in the field and Morrissey's big fists again were put to use. If he wasn't fighting for business reasons any other excuse would do. Once it was a woman, one Kate Ridgely, a lady of the bagnios. He came to blows with Tom McCann, another noted bruiser, over the somewhat doubtful affections of this soiled dove. It was in a saloon and the two of them knocked over a stove in the scuffle. The hot coals fell out and Mr. McCann chivalrously rolled Morrissey into them. But in spite of that he won.

Victories with his knuckles had, by this time, given Morrissey considerable political standing among those who wanted rough work done. But they had earned him little money. Empty of pocket, he was fairly easy prey for the gold-fever germ and in 1851 went to California to seek his fortune. He didn't find it underground. But he did make the discovery that he could capitalize his great gnarled fists.

He made his début as a professional fighter at Mare Island, gaining $2,000 by winning from George Thompson on a foul in the eleventh round. The money took him back to New York where he gathered up another goodly sum by defeating that swashbuckling bully, Yankee Sullivan, in thirty-seven rounds at Boston Four Corners, a hideaway one hundred miles northeast of New York.

During all this time he did not neglect his street fighting, which was a labor of love. He never lost an opportunity to stage a brawl. More often he provoked such parties. Once he almost became involved in serious difficulties. He was a participant in the little unpleasantness that resulted in the murder of "Butcher Bill" Poole, a prominent barbarian, in 1854, and only political pull snatched him from the shadow of the law.

Eventually he achieved the pugilistic pinnacle. In 1858, for the championship of everything in sight, he defeated John C. Heenan, an old enemy from the streets of Troy, knocking him endwise in the eighteenth round of a savage battle at Long Island Point, a spot on Lake Erie not far from Buffalo.

With this he retired from the ring. Nor could he be coaxed back. Heenan begged for another match but could not get it. Great purses were offered for a battle between Morrissey and Tom Sayers, the champion of England, but Morrissey had promised his bride he would not fight again and he kept his word.

Morrissey had gambled in his time and had been smart enough to learn that the odds were with the house. He took his earnings of the prize ring and started a small faro-bank establishment on Broadway, near Great Jones Street. Faro was the great game of the day and so popular that gaming-house owners did not need to be dishonest to make money. Morrissey soon had several establishments and a small fortune.

In 1861 he branched out on a grand scale. Saratoga Springs was the East's great resort. Morrissey opened a modest gambling house there by way of feeling his way

[87]

and soon was so firmly entrenched politically that he built the Saratoga Club House, a toll booth of great luxury which later was operated by Richard Canfield. Not long afterward he added a racetrack. He became a power. He ran an honest game, too, and Saratoga became as famous a gambling resort as Baden Baden and Monte Carlo on another continent.

Then ambition again took hold of Morrissey. It was the old urge to fight but by this time his knuckles were of little use to him. He chose the field of politics, in which he already was a familiar figure. He still had a following from his early days.

He put gambling behind him as a business and, under the Tammany banner, was twice elected to Congress. He was a good Congressman, too, it is recorded, according to his lights; good enough to break with Tammany in its wicked days and fight Tweed with all the rough cunning he had learned on the docks and in the ring.

At the very height of his career he came a cropper in the field of finance. He had met many notables in his gambling establishments. One of these was old Commodore Vanderbilt, and it was he who induced Morrissey to take a flier in Wall Street. There are some who believe the Commodore took him for a ride. At any rate he was clipped for a large sum in the Vanderbilt railroad stocks before he knew what it was all about.

His fortune gone, his great frame weakened by punishment and excesses, Morrissey began to lose his grip. He didn't give up without a struggle, though. When the finish came in 1878 he was fighting away with white gloves over his rough fists. It was a battle with Tammany for a state senatorship. It must have been the last source of satisfaction to him to know that he had won. But he never collected this last purse, for before the legislature convened he had taken the longest of counts.

SMOKE AT SEA

Chapter XII: Smoke at Sea

IT WAS John Fitch, a gaunt, frustrated genius, who invented the steamboat. He died a suicide. Robert Fulton, a New York dilettante, came along with a later model, cruised it on the Hudson, and won the credit along with wealth.

The most that can be said for Fulton, however, is that he invented the Albany night-boat. His *Clermont* dared not poke its nose into the open sea that stretched between the Old World and the New. For years steamboats were content to hug the shore, if they ventured out of inland waters at all. They braved Long Island Sound but only for short trips and most of these within the sight of land.

Eventually, of course, they conquered the ocean and brought Europe within commuting distance. For this Captain Moses Rogers, a mariner of the old school, whose imagination was stronger than the wind that was depended on to fill the sails of the packets of his day, is to be thanked.

Captain Rogers had put out of his home port, New London, Conn., as a youth and had traveled the seas for years under sail. When Fulton, at the turn of the Nineteenth Century, backed by the money Fitch could not raise, set out in earnest to prove his contention that ships could be propelled by steam most of the old-line mariners scoffed. Captain Rogers was not among the number.

Instead, he cast his lot with the dreamer and when the *Clermont* started up the

Hudson on that memorable day in 1807 he was not one of those who lined the shore in the firm belief they would see the vessel blown to bits. He was on the bridge contributing the knowledge of an old salt to the success of the experiment.

Later he commanded the *Phœnix* when it tried its steam power against the ocean. It wasn't much of a trip—from Sandy Hook to Cape May—and it could hardly have been called a great success for a storm almost blew the paddle wheel away before he could beach the craft. But the skipper was convinced that he could cross the ocean with the new power.

Shipping men did not share his confidence. For almost a decade he sought his chance in vain. Eventually persistence was rewarded. Savannah, Ga., at that time was a thriving port. Its business men were of the type now termed "go-getters" and the daring of Captain Rogers appealed to them. They saw an opportunity to advertise their city. Under the leadership of Scarborough & Isaacs, a shipping firm, they clubbed together and provided funds for the adventure.

A ship already under construction at Corlear's Hook in New York was purchased. It was to have been a sailing vessel but Captain Rogers arrived upon the scene in time to make a change or two. When the *Savannah*, as its sponsors named it, slid into the water it was full-rigged, except that there were no sails loftier than topgallant, but it obviously was not an ordinary clipper.

Its mainmaist and its foremast were quite far apart. Between them, in the unusually wide space, lay its boilers and its ninety-horsepower engine. On its side was a paddle wheel of eight radial arms. Curiously enough this paddle wheel was so constructed that it could be taken apart and hauled aboard. Captain Rogers was not so brave as he might have been. If he met stormy weather he planned to pull his wheel in and depend upon the well-tried canvas.

[92]

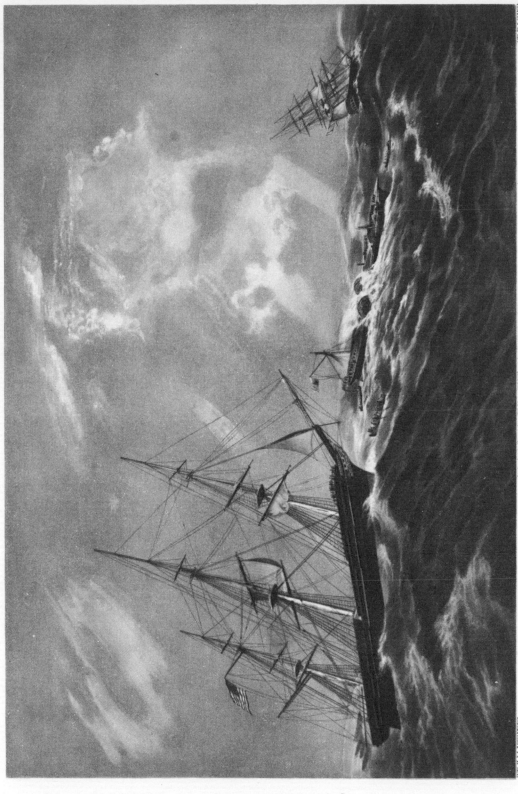

ANTARCTIC.

THREE BELLS

PAINT. BY F.F. PALMER.

LITH. BY N CURRIER

The ships ANTARCTIC of New York, CAPT STOUFFER, and THREE BELLS of Glasgow, CAPT CREIGHTON, rescuing the passengers and crew from

THE WRECK OF THE STEAM SHIP "SAN FRANCISCO."

DISABLED ON HER VOYAGE FROM NEW YORK TO SAN FRANCISCO DEC. 24TH 1853 AND IN A SINKING CONDITION.

The Bark KILBY, of Boston, CAPT. LOW, had previously fallen in with the wreck, and taken off a part of the passengers, but during a gale in the night was separated and could not regain it.

NEW YORK. PUBLISHED BY N CURRIER, 152 NASSAU STREET.

THE MAMMOTH IRON STEAM-SHIP "GREAT EASTERN" 22,500 TONS, 3000 HORSE POWER.

LENGTH 680 FEET (OVER ⅛ OF A MILE.)
BREADTH 83 FT.
FOUR DECKS.
18,915 TONS REGISTER.
5000 TONS LARGER THAN NOAH'S ARK.
DRAUGHT OF WATER 20 FT
& WHEN LADEN 30 FT

Designed by J. K. Brunel, Esq. F.R.S. Built by Mess.rs Scott
Russell, London. Weight of Iron used in the construction 10,000
Tons. Combined Steam power 3000 horses & spreads 6,500 square
Yards of canvas. To walk round the Deck exceeds ⅛ of mile.

DIAMETER OF SIDE WHEELS 60 FT
DIAMETER OF SCREW PROPELLER 24 FT
DEPTH FROM DECK TO HOLD 60 FT
WILL CARRY 10,000 TROOPS OR
800 FIRST CLASS
2000 SECOND D.o } Total 4000.
1200 THIRD D.o

52 NASSAU S.t NEW Y.

To-day the *Savannah* would be just a dot upon the ocean. It was of only 350 tons burthen. It had thirty-two staterooms and two salons, "one for the ladies and one for the gents," and it was furnished "elegantly" with "magnificent imported carpets, curtains, hangings and mirrors." Captain Rogers was assured that it would do ten knots under canvas. What it would do under steam was anybody's guess.

It sailed from New York for its home port on the morning of March 29, 1819. The writer of its log says it did not "git up steam" until the next day. It arrived in Savannah April 6th, with a good deal of cheering. President Monroe and his Cabinet made a trip to inspect it, although there were those who urged the President not to go aboard for fear he might be killed by an explosion.

There was a big banquet at which many speeches were made. And then the toast—"The Constitution of the United States—framed by the wisdom of sages—may our statesmen and posterity regard it as the national ark of political safety never to be abandoned"—was drunk with all standing.

The *Savannah* was scheduled to embark upon its transatlantic voyage May 20th. However, it did not get away on that date. In the manner of a Coney Island bus it lingered waiting for passengers. But it waited in vain. Every sort of ballyhoo was tried but it was no use. No one could be found who was willing to chance the ocean with steam. Two days later it shoved off without a single passenger and without an ounce of freight.

Mr. Marconi not yet having thought of the wireless, there was no news of the ship for several days. Then the schooner *Contract* put into New York. The skipper was a little upset. He reported that a day or two before he had seen a ship on fire at sea. He had set about to rescue it.

[93]

"But the damn thing wouldn't stop," he blustered, "and we couldn't catch up with her."

He felt better when he heard the explanation. But the *Savannah* ran into the same experience when it arrived off Cork on June 17th, belching smoke. The admiral of the British fleet dispatched one of the King's cutters to put out the blaze. Captain Rogers reported back that his craft was not afire. But the British insisted on going aboard and seeing for themselves.

The ship went on to Liverpool, completing its crossing in twenty-nine days and eleven hours. It had used steam only eighty hours of the way but it had proved that waves could be bucked without sails. In Liverpool the *Savannah* created something of a stir. It was thought that the craft was on its way to St. Helena to rescue Napoleon. But the skipper cleared himself of the suspicion.

On July 23d the vessel continued on its way, calling first at Copenhagen and then at Stockholm. In the Swedish port it finally picked up a passenger. Lord Lynedock, a British peer with the spirit of adventure, booked the very best stateroom and proceeded with the craft to Cronstadt. When he landed there he was so pleased with his jaunt that he presented Captain Rogers with a solid silver teakettle and made a little speech.

"I blame no man born in the United States for being proud of his country," he said. "If I was a young man I would go there myself."

From Cronstadt Captain Rogers and his crew were taken to St. Petersburg, which since has become Leningrad. There they were fêted. The captain was presented with a gold snuff box by the Czar himself.

The *Savannah* started back on October 10th. Five days later it called at Elsinore, Hamlet's home town, and then at Arendale, Norway. Then it took to the open sea once more. It had refueled abroad but to little advantage. The weather was so stormy all the way back that Captain Rogers hauled in his precious paddle wheel at the start and didn't use it until he was just outside Savannah.

The ship made its home port again on November 13th. But with just one fare collected, and that for a short run, its sponsors were hardly to be blamed for coming to the conclusion that steamships were not meant for the ocean. They tore the engine out of the hull, discarded the paddle wheel, replaced the missing sails, and put the vessel into the coastwise service between their Georgia port and New York. On November 5, 1821, it headed into a storm it could not weather and sank off Moriches, L. I.

For many years the lesson of the *Savannah* was enough for American shippers. As a matter of fact it was the British who finally perfected the steamship for ocean travel. The first vessel to cross the Atlantic using only steam power was the *Royal William*, which made the trip from Quebec to London in 1833.

Five years later the steamship *Sirius*, equipped with a sturdy engine and side wheels, came into New York harbor and the very next day the *Great Western* arrived. From that time on the ocean was dotted with smoking craft. The Cunard Line, subsidized by the British government, sent most of them back and forth. There were the *Asia* and the *Africa* and the *Scotia* and the *British Queen* and the *Britannia* and the *President*.

Perhaps the finest of the pioneer steamships was the *Great Eastern*. No longer ship sailed the seas until the *Oceanic* was launched in 1899 and none was wider until the *Mauretania* was built. But the *Great Eastern* was too big for her time. The cost of operation was enormous and the Eastern Navigation Company, which built her, went to the wall because of her.

It was many years before the steamships could compete with the clipper ships of the '50s for speed. But eventually their engines were perfected and men who were accustomed to driving their way across the ocean with sails learned how to get results from the power that Jimmy Watt found in a teakettle. Now, of course, they do very well.

TO MARKET, TO MARKET, TO BUY A FINE STOCK

Chapter XIII: *To Market, To Market, To Buy a Fine Stock*

THE Revolution which created the United, as the saying goes, States of America created also Wall Street, a fact which may or may not be in fulfillment of the law of compensations.

The thoroughfare itself had threaded its narrow way across the nether end of Manhattan Island many years before the Colonies challenged their king. But it was not yet paved with gold and greed. It had taken its name and its form from a stockade built in 1643 by the Dutch, to discourage visits from Indians seized with homicidal mania. When the spreading city pushed past the boundary line Wall Street became a business thoroughfare of importance.

In due time came the insurrection. Money was needed to finance it. Taxation was a bothersome process. And so the Continental government, not burdened with too many scruples, simply issued paper currency regardless of its ability to redeem it. Solvency was a distant dream when peace came. "Not worth a continental," referred to the impotence of this scrip in post-Revolutionary days,

It was the belief of Alexander Hamilton that to establish American credit these securities must be redeemed at par. When he was made Secretary of the Treasury he set about to achieve this end and, in the process, he created America's first specula-

[99]

tive boom. Wise men, with the knowledge of his plan as an ace in the hole, sent their agents out to buy up all the paper money they could get. Those who held it, and had tried to cash it, considered it worthless and were glad to sell for fifteen cents on the dollar. Even after Congress had approved Hamilton's plan the news was slow reaching some parts of the country and agents, riding ahead of it on horses and ships, bought without risk.

This was the first "bull" market. Some of the American fortunes that are not yet fully spent were founded in this way. The wise merchants and brokers of Wall Street had foreseen the possibilities and had formed syndicates to carry on a business in currency. The thoroughfare had had its taste of easy money.

It was another of Hamilton's projects that fanned the flames. He organized the National Bank and its stock was soon soaring. Members of Congress had allotted to themselves some of the shares. Friends of Hamilton had acquired their portion. Wily bankers and brokers picked it up at par. The public began to clamor for it. By August 1791 it was selling for 195. And then the wise men sold. A month later it was quoted at 108.

This time there was trouble. One or two financial houses failed. Old Pierre de Peyster rode his horse down Wall Street and demanded his money back from Colonel William Duer. He got it, but few of the other investors were wise enough to take their pistols with them when they made their demands, and so they lost out.

These two incidents had given evidence of the public's willingness to risk its money. Auctioneers dealing in stocks had sprung up on Wall Street. There were independent brokers, too, and they gathered under a great buttonwood tree in front of 68 Wall Street each day to compare notes and prices. Eventually, to protect themselves, they organized—twenty-four of them. That was on May 17, 1792, and it was

Entered according to Act of Congress in the year 1849 by N. Currier, in the Clerk's office of the District Court of the Southern District of N. Y.

STOCKS UP.

Entered according to Act of Congress in the year 1849 by N. Currier, in the Clerk's office of the District Court of the southern District of N. Y.

STOCKS DOWN.

the beginning of the Stock Exchange. Twenty years later they left the shade of their tree and moved indoors at 40 Wall Street.

But for years the Stock Exchange was without drama. It was no more exciting than a country store. Brokers did nothing more than buy and sell stocks for a commission. Their list grew with the development of banks and factories and railroads but trading was a dull business. On the average day a few thousand dollars would have bought all the stocks traded in.

Then came the panic of 1837 and with it Wall Street's first schemer. It was Jacob Little, a rangy man with fever in his eyes, who discovered that he could manipulate the market. He sensed the approaching debacle and became the first "bear." He originated the "short" sale—disposing freely of stocks he did not own and driving the prices down to a point at which he could acquire them.

Quite naturally he was considered an agent of Satan himself and every effort was made to ruin him. Three times he was driven to bankruptcy and each time he came back. Once he sold more Erie stock than could be bought and Wall Street believed he was done for. But he sent to England, picked up a number of convertible bonds and made his deliveries. Finally, however, he plunged too far and was wrecked.

Little changed the entire aspect of stock trading. There followed in his wake bulls and bears who, from time to time, have made Wall Street either a dazzling thoroughfare paved with gold or a drab little lane leading to a cemetery. It became a battlefield for daring men.

Its first great struggle for personal supremacy was between Commodore Cornelius Vanderbilt and Daniel Drew, in the '50s. Vanderbilt, a Staten Island farm boy, founded his fortune with money he earned by plying a small boat as a ferry between Staten Island and New York. Drew began as a drover. His first coup came with stock rather than stocks. On the way to New York with a load of cattle he realized they were too lean to get good prices. He camped in the Harlem Valley and scattered salt on the ground. The cattle ate and thirsted and drank. When they reached New York they were fat and valuable. From this trick comes the expression "watered stock."

Vanderbilt was a natural bull, Drew a bear. For years they ruled Wall Street between them, with first one triumphant and then the other. They played with great industries to satisfy their own greeds and grudges. They jockeyed the financial markets of the nation until a dark-skinned, dark-eyed young man named Jay Gould came down from upstate with fewer scruples than either of them and beat them at their own ruthless game.

Gould it was who brought about "Black Friday," the darkest day Wall Street has ever known. With the aid of that simple and grotesque mountebank, "Jubilee Jim" Fisk, he had built up a new system of manipulation in which judges and legislatures were bought and sold along with stocks. He even attempted to take a President into his camp in his conspiracy to corner the gold market. But Grant was too naïve for him, the scheme failed, and Friday, October 4, 1869, was black with ruin and suicide.

There were other colorful plungers in Wall Street, of course—Jay Cooke, Jim Keene, Leonard Jerome, "Bet-a-million" Gates—but eventually the organization of "big business," by which industrial control was centralized, left them a smaller field in which to operate. Now Wall Street's structure is safe against the manipulative attacks of the few. It is, however, still the world's largest green-baize table.

HALF AND HALF

Chapter XIV: Half and Half

IN THE memoirs of midgets there is, perhaps, no more curious story than the romance of Tom Thumb and Lavinia Warren. Tom Thumb was twenty-five inches tall, Lavinia Warren, twenty-four. They loved, they married, and, for all the world ever knew, they lived happily ever afterward, which, as any cynic will tell you, is more than many a couple of normal attainments has done.

Inasmuch as all this devotion flowered under the benign auspices of the shrewdest of all showmen, Mr. P. T. Barnum, who delighted in the title "Prince of Humbugs," the temptation has been to class it with the spurious phenomena for which he was famous—the Feejee mermaid, the cherry-colored cat, the woolly horse. But there is evidence to the contrary, evidence which entitles the two to their place in authentic amatory chronicles along with full-blown beaux and belles.

Mysterious glandular processes, not even yet entirely clear to science, made Tom Thumb and Lavinia Warren microscopic. It was Mr. Barnum who made them much larger in the public eye than most of us will ever be.

The showman discovered Charles S. Stratton playing on the streets of Bridgeport, Conn. He was just five years old and obviously had completed his growth, such as it was. Barnum saw the possibilities of exploitation at once, bustled the dapperling off to his museum in New York at three dollars a week, added six years to his age overnight, rechristened him "General Tom Thumb," and announced that he had "just arrived from England."

Tom was a bright, pink-cheeked pigwidgeon, neither grotesque nor malformed. He had a wit of his own, too, which enabled him to form his own answers to questions and to take direction from Mr. Barnum after the manner of a real actor. He told stories well and he sang songs amusingly. He caught the public imagination immediately.

When, two years later, Mr. Barnum took him off to Europe his popularity was such that ten thousand people waved him farewell from the pier and the city sent its own brass band to bludgeon the air. In London Queen Victoria found him something at which she *could* be amused; in Paris, where he was known as Le Général Tom Pouce, Louis Philippe gave him an audience and a diamond brooch; and in Madrid Queen Isabella took him to a bull fight.

He returned to even greater triumphs at home. He did not labor long for the three-dollar weekly wage Mr. Barnum paid him at the start but proved so good a business man that he soon had money in many banks, ponies and yachts, and valuable real estate in Bridgeport, including a house of his own built to his size and furnished in his abbreviated proportions.

Lavinia Warren was born Mercy Lavinia Warren Bumpus in Middleboro, Mass., and stopped growing shortly thereafter. At twenty-one she had attained her full height of twenty-four inches and was sensitive about it. She was teaching school when a shrewd Yankee relative convinced her that she could capitalize her inconsiderability and see the world. It was the thought of travel that lured her and she started trouping. She hadn't gone far before Mr. Barnum discovered her and took her to New York.

By this time Tom Thumb had grown a little pudgy and so wealthy that he could do as he pleased. He preferred to play with his ponies and his yacht in Bridgeport so Mr. Barnum had to find himself another elf. This he did in George Washington Morrison Nutt, a youth of nineteen who towered to twenty-nine inches.

The showman transferred his allegiance to the navy this time and called his new find "Commodore" Nutt. The Commodore was a bit of a ladies' man and it wasn't long before he was emotionally aware of the presence in the museum of Miss Warren. He became an ardent, if infinitesimal, cavalier.

All might have gone well if Tom Thumb had not dropped down from Bridgeport one day to smell the grease paint once again. He was introduced to Miss Warren, talked to her for a few minutes, and then, by the process of tugging at the gentleman's coat tails, got Mr. Barnum into his private office and closed the door.

"Mr. Barnum," he announced with all the fervor of which he was capable, "that is the most charming lady I ever saw, and I believe that she was created on purpose to be my wife."

The Prince of Humbugs was no fool and probably saw the possibilities at once. But he did not have to do Tom Thumb's courting for him. Indeed, the young man spent so much time at the museum that Commodore Nutt soon became jealous. He made no effort to conceal his resentment and, on one occasion, provoked a quarrel and knocked the General flat on the floor, which wasn't far away.

From that moment, Mr. Thumb planned his campaign with considerable cunning and eventually went to Mr. Barnum with the request that he invite Miss Warren to the Barnum home in Bridgeport for a week-end so that he might propose. The

Commodore got wind of the invitation and persuaded Mr. Barnum to ask him, too. But Miss Warren was given Saturday off and the Commodore was forced to remain in New York until after the seven-thirty show at the museum.

The General met his lady at the station with his miniature coach-and-four and spent the day showing her the real estate he owned. After dinner at the Barnum home the host feigned a tactful yawn and went off to bed. Two young ladies of the household, however, were not so polite. They hid on the stairway and listened.

It seems that the General began by explaining, in a nice way, how rich he was. He exhibited bank books, property deeds, and insurance policies. Eventually he brought up the fact that Miss Warren was soon to leave for Europe. He told her of his own travels abroad and said that if he were to go along he could explain things to her. Miss Warren said that would be nice.

"Don't you think it would be nicer if we went as man and wife?" asked Mr. Thumb, putting his arm around her waist.

Miss Warren said she didn't know. And removed the arm. The General didn't bother with further questioning on the point but reached over and kissed her. By the time the Commodore arrived they were engaged. They didn't get a chance to tell him. He was so angry at Mr. Barnum for leaving them alone that he went off to wake the gentleman and give him a piece of his mind.

The wedding took place in Grace Church, N. Y., February 10, 1863. Mr. Barnum didn't dare sell tickets. The two thousand guests were all invited and included governors, congressmen, army and navy officers, and representatives of the best families. President Lincoln sent his regrets and a set of Chinese fire screens.

A platform was built in front of the altar so that the principals might be seen by the throng. Commodore Nutt, still pouting, was the best man, and Minnie

GEN'L TOM THUMB & WIFE, COMM'DT & MINNIE WARREN,

FOUR WONDROUSLY FORMED & STRANGELY BEAUTIFUL LADIES & GENTLEMEN IN MINIATURES, NATURES SMALLEST EDITIONS OF HER CHOICEST WORKS.

THE GREATEST WONDERS IN THE WORLD.

A MARRIED COUPLE, A BACHELOR & A BELLE, ALL FOUR WEIGHING BUT 100 POUNDS. They are all perfect in development educated & intelligent, and fitted, both intellectually & physically, for all the duties & requirements of life. Robust health, beauty, grace, manly dignity & feminine sweetness are combined in them in the amplest manner. No Exhibition more Marvelously beautiful was ever known or seen—viz:

SPLENDID EQUIPAGE OF GEN'L TOM THUMB & SUITE, COST OVER $2000.

GEN'L TOM THUMB'S MARRIAGE AT GRACE CHURCH, N.Y. FEB'Y 10th 1863.

Warren, the bride's tiny sister, the maid of honor. It was only at the last minute that Bishop Potter declined to perform the ceremony. Mr. Barnum got two ministers to replace him.

There was a honeymoon and then, later, a tour of Europe and the Orient. Eventually Mr. and Mrs. Tom Thumb settled down. A child was born to them but lived only two years. The General himself, plump with good living, died in 1883. Lavinia later married Count Primo Magri, an Italian dwarf, and the two of them ran a country store in Massachusetts until her death in 1919.

THE ICE AGE

Chapter XV: The Ice Age

AS A matter of fact, where *are* the snows of yesteryear? The tiresome old gentleman who, at the drop of a flake, recounts the bitter story of the blizzard of '88 is right when he says that winters are not what they used to be. At least he is right so far as New York is concerned. No one drives to work in a sleigh any more. And if you see a man with skates over his shoulder you may be fairly sure he is bound for St. Moritz and not Central Park.

Scientists and pseudo-scientists have various explanations. The simplest seems the most logical. New York now has a population of 7,000,000 souls. Each has an average temperature of 98.4. Their combined heat is enough to melt a glacier. Add to this the warmth thrown out by furnaces and other heating systems. It is not surprising that sleighbells are stilled and skates are rusted.

However, there was a time when winter was a season in New York. It began, really, with the first flurry of snow, a visitation which never took the gay bloods of the town by surprise. They watched for it from the moment frost appeared. They kept their cutters ready. As soon as it was thick enough upon the ground they were out and the race was on—for Gabe Case, who ran a roadhouse on "the road" up above McComb's Dam, gave a magnum of champagne to the first to reach his hospice in a sleigh.

With that moment the winter pageant began. As soon as they could finish their daily tasks men hitched their horses, tucked buffalo robes or sealskin mantles about their womenfolk, and drove their cutters into the winter. The most famous trotters of the town took their places on the white carpeted road alongside nags that had pulled milk wagons all day. It wasn't speed that counted in the snow. It was endurance. And the music of bells drowned the sound of the most ungainly hoofs.

With the first freeze, too, a red ball was hung from an old tower near the reservoir in Central Park. There were no towering buildings then to obscure the view and it could be seen from almost every part of the town. It meant that the lake was frozen over and ready for skating. The red ball was the signal for every beau and his belle. The lake took on the appearance of a Russian fair.

For the belle it was an opportunity to appear at her best. Rouge had not yet made its appearance. Red cheeks were made by wintry air. There is a story of the age of innocence which illustrates the point. A very young lady, it seems, remarked that she was sweating.

"Only animals sweat," said her mother, with the proper tone of disapproval. "Men sometimes perspire. Girls glow, my dear."

And so the girls took on a thoroughly proper glow. How they managed much agility in their sweeping skirts is beyond modern understanding. The audacious swain welcomed winter because it gave him an opportunity to put on his lady's skates and perhaps catch a glimpse of her ankle.

When the frost nipped a nose there was a spacious clubhouse and a great cast-iron stove, white with heat to the point of seeming porcelain. And perhaps an oyster stew.

There were other places to skate, too. At times the Hudson River would freeze its width and skaters would be able to journey to New Jersey and back. One year it was so popular for parties that a bright young man set up a tent restaurant on the ice. He did a thriving business until his stove became too hot. Then it disappeared and he with it. Rescuers fished him out of the hole it had melted in the ice.

These early skaters may have been gay but they could not have been graceful. They used, for the most part, the short, choppy strokes of the Dutch, who had introduced the pastime to America.

As a matter of fact they rejected their first opportunity to acquire grace and beauty on the ice. It was offered by a young man named Jackson Haines, a ballet master who took to skates after being educated abroad for the theater. He had a curious notion that he could transplant the waltz and the mazurka and other rhythms to ice and, after assiduous practice, he succeeded in doing so.

But the American skaters were content with their less fluent style and would have none of the hard work of changing it. Haines, rebuffed, packed up his skates and went to Europe. There he was received with open arms. In the '60s he made triumphant appearances in all the Continental capitals with tremendous success.

Not only could he dance on ice. He mastered other tricks few skaters before him or after him could achieve. He practiced for a full year before he accomplished a spin on bended knee. He was the only skater who ever succeeded in finishing the figure by skating a triple spiral out from the center of rotation. He was a bit of a showman, too. He always managed to lose his cap while executing a difficult figure and to pick it up without stopping.

It was Haines who created figure skating in its modern sense. He gave it to Europe, without ever returning to America. At an ice festival on the Neva in Russia and before the appreciative eyes of Czar Alexander II he executed all his most difficult stunts and then, in a simple trick of jumping over a chair, he fell and broke his leg. That ended his skating career. Several years afterward he died in a little town in Finland.

Years later an American, Irving Brokaw, discovered his grave there marked simply: "The American Skating King." It was Brokaw, too, who discovered in Europe the system of figure skating Haines had taken abroad. He brought it back to America. It thrives to-day in New York but to a great extent on the ice man manufactures to take the place of that which his own heat prevents from forming naturally.

CENTRAL-PARK, WINTER.

THE SKATING POND.

Entered according to Act of Congress in the Year 1864, by Currier & Ives, in the Clerk's Office of the District Court of the United States for the Southern District of New York.

NEW YORK, PUBLISHED BY CURRIER & IVES, 152 NASSAU ST.

CASEY JONES'S PROFESSION

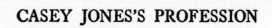

Chapter XVI: Casey Jones's Profession

RAILWAYS had their beginning in England as nothing more than planked wagon ruts in the roads from the Newcastle mines to the sea. By the time the idea reached America, probably along with a shipload of coal, it had had the benefit of improvements. And so when Gridley Bryant played the pioneer here in 1826 he built real rails with fine pine timber and faced them with bar iron.

This first railway of the very new republic covered the three miles between Mr. Bryant's granite quarries near Quincy, Mass., and the Neponset River. Horses hauled the cars, which were nothing more than wagons, from the river to the quarries. The return trip was left largely to gravity and the proper grade. The wagons, loaded with granite for the Bunker Hill Monument in Boston, rolled down to the river at a speed of four and a half miles an hour. The horses, not being fools, rode with them.

Mr. Bryant's railway cost about fifty thousand dollars and paid for itself by reducing his transportation cost to one sixth what it had been. But he was not the only one to profit. The innovation was widely publicized and tourists came from all parts of the country to see how it worked. A wily Yankee of the neighborhood turned his house into an inn and with this trade alone was able to retire with considerable wealth before the public curiosity was satisfied.

It was this curiosity, incidentally, which caused the first railroad accident a year or two later. The line had not been designed for carrying passengers and made no attempt to do so. But a group of sightseers from Baltimore could not resist the temptation of climbing aboard. Halfway up the chain broke, and the car ran away and toppled over a forty-foot cliff. One of the men was killed and the rest severely injured.

Other railroads popped up in various parts of the country soon after. The cars were all drawn by horses or mules until England presented the world with the steam engine. A gentleman named Horatio Allen, acting for the Delaware & Hudson Canal Company, which had decided to forestall competition by having a railroad of its own, imported four of these in 1829.

Allen selected one of them, named "The Stourbridge Lion," for a demonstration on rails that had been built from the mines at Carbondale, Pa., to the canal terminal at Honesdale. A holiday was declared, a large crowd gathered, a gentleman blew his arm off trying to fire a cannon by way of salute, and Mr. Allen drove his engine five or six miles. There was more cheering than the occasion warranted, for the experiment proved the engines unsuited to the road and they were abandoned.

America produced a steam engine of its own in 1830. It was called, with a trace of sentiment, "The Best Friend of Charleston," and it resembled nothing so much as a large catsup bottle on wheels. However, it proved, under trial, to be capable of doing twenty-one miles an hour. It might have done better had it not come to an untimely end. A negro fireman, not being entirely familiar with its ways, became annoyed at the noise made by escaping steam and by way of achieving quiet sat on the valve. The subsequent explosion sped the gentleman to Mr. Casey Jones's promised land faster than "The Best Friend of Charleston" could have taken him— and left the engine a wreck.

By this time the Baltimore & Ohio, the first of America's great contributions to the railways of the world, was well under way. Baltimore had become alarmed at the inland trade that had gone to New York through the recently completed Erie Canal. Its public-spirited citizens had provided funds for a railroad that would get somewhere.

But the Baltimore & Ohio ran into power trouble at the start. Locomotives were considered unsafe for curves, of which there were a great many in the roadbed that was being built westward. Cars with huge sails were tried. They worked beautifully when the wind was high. But the wind had a way of dying down. Horse-propelled treadmills were used until one day one of the horses saw a cow and bolted.

And then Peter Cooper, an inventive genius, was drawn into the railway project indirectly. He had been induced by two men to join them in buying some land along the proposed line for the purposes of speculation. His partners sent him no profits. Instead they dunned him frequently for assessments. He became suspicious and, investigating, found that he was being swindled.

By this time Mr. Cooper owned so much property that he stood to lose a great deal of money if the railroad plan failed. And he perceived at once that it would fail if it did not have locomotives that could take curves. So he went back to his foundry in New York and started to work. By one or two ingenious strokes, including the use of musket barrels for boiler tubes, he turned out an engine known as the "Tom Thumb" which took the curves and saved the railroad.

The "Tom Thumb" was capable of fair speed, too, although one of its early experiences was humiliating. Shortly after it had startled the natives with its dazzling performances it was challenged by an old gray mare. The mare was off to a good lead but the engine soon passed her. And then, with triumph near, the blower belt slipped. Cooper himself was at the helm. He tried to keep steam up by hand but it died down and the mare sped on to victory.

The defeat was no great blow. however, to the development of locomotives. They soon proved they could beat horses. As early as 1838 demonstrations of speed were taking place. In that year a record was made for the dispatch of news. By special arrangement with the government a tried and true conductor was given a copy of a Presidential message immediately after it had been delivered. He rushed in a hansom cab to the station in Washington, boarded his train, and the news was in Baltimore in one hour and eighteen minutes. It was relayed on to Philadelphia and New York in record time and the nation marveled.

When the West had shown itself to be not one but several gold mines clamor for a transcontinental railway arose. Those who started the hue did not remain to see it through. There was Asa Whitney, for instance, who stumped the country urging the plan. But his campaign cost so much that he had to go back to peddling milk for a living before the idea actually took form.

It was first suggested as a government project and thus came into the realm of politics. Candidates rose and fell on the issue. And, as is customary even in our present-day politics, nothing really happened. Great plans were made on paper and long speeches were made in Congress. But that was all.

Mr. Kipling had not yet made his discouraging remark to the effect that East is East and West is West and never the twain shall meet, so, eventually, the West started out to meet the East. Ground was broken at Sacramento on January 8, 1863, and the Central Pacific Railroad was under way.

It was no simple task. In the first place there was the labor problem. Californians had not yet been cured of the gold fever. Men who were strong enough for rough work preferred to gamble in the mines. Those in charge of construction found that as soon as a workman had earned enough on the railroad to enable him to go prospecting he dropped his pick and his shovel and went off in quest of gold.

It was the far-seeing Charles Crocker who met the situation by importing Chinese clear across the Pacific Ocean. Not only would they work cheaply but they had no get-rich-quick notions and were quite content to hold to the task of pushing the rails eastward. By the time the road was completed more than ten thousand Chinese had been put to work. Mr. Crocker said later that he employed them originally because he felt sure that any race that could build the wall of China could force a railroad through mountains.

Meantime the East had started out to meet the West, too. In 1865, ground was broken at Omaha, Neb., for the Union Pacific Railroad. Ox teams trundled out from Chicago with materials for the great drive and soon rails were being laid and the prairies were being skimmed.

But the Union Pacific had its troubles, too. It was difficult to get supplies to the large army of men it employed. Half the time many of them were required to live on the game of the country in which they happened to be working. Indeed, on more than one occasion a hunter was assigned as a regular member of a gang and it was his duty to go out each day and bag enough to feed the men of the outfit. Even with game plentiful it was no easy job, for working on the railroad made stout appetites.

Then there was the Indian. The Indian, oddly enough, resented the intrusion of

[123]

"the iron horse." Red hordes frequently swept down on the workmen and thinned their ranks. Not a little old-fashioned scalping took place. The question of how to work and fight at the same time soon became a serious one.

Eventually the government helped to solve it. A military escort of ten or twenty men was assigned to each gang. The workmen themselves were drilled and armed. Most of them had had Civil War experience and knew what it was all about.

The members of the military escort would take their places each morning on such promontories as the working field provided. There they would remain all day watching for skulking redskins. When they would see dust clouds thrown up by flying heels they would rush back to the working camp, line up their men, and prepare to fight for their lives. Frequently they lost. But the railroad pushed on.

Finally the two lines—the one from the West and the other from the East—drew near to each other in Utah, so near in fact that there was rivalry between the workmen. The Union Pacific's gangs were composed largely of Irishmen. They resented the fact that Chinese were building the Central Pacific. Once or twice they overloaded their blasts and blew rocks at "the Chinks." But this did not last long. The yellow men knew how to fight, too. They used blasts, also, and one day almost buried "the Micks" under rocks. From then on the relations were less strained.

As the two roads neared each other the government took a hand in the situation and notified the officials that they would have to link their lines at a spot called Promontory Point, near the northern end of the Great Salt Lake. Here the East and the West met on May 10, 1869—seven years before the time set for the completion of the lines.

It was a great occasion and one that was celebrated by all who could get to the out-of-the-way point. The last tie was placed under the rails and a prayer was

THE "LIGHTNING EXPRESS" TRAINS.

"Leaving the Junction"

NEW YORK, PUBLISHED BY CURRIER & IVES, 152 NASSAU STREET.

AMERICAN EXPRESS TRAIN.

JOHN A.ROEBLING, ESQ. ENGINEER,

C. PARSONS, DEL.

THE RAIL ROAD SUSPENSION BRIDGE,

NEAR NIAGARA FALLS.

Length of Bridge 822 feet. Height above Water 240 feet.

NEW YORK, PUBLISHED BY CURRIER & IVES 152 NASSAU STREET.

Entered according to Act of Congress in the year 1856 by N Currier, in the Clerks Office of the District Court of the Southern District of N.Y.

offered. Then a spike of solid gold—the last to be driven—was put into place. Officials of the two roads were given sledges. But they were so nervous that none of them hit the spike in the first four or five attempts but almost ruined the tie with their whacks. Each blow, as it was struck, was telegraphed to all parts of the country.

Then two engines were brought forth—one headed east and the other west. They chugged slowly along the tracks until they gently bumped noses at the point of intersection. Each engineer at this point leaned out of his cab and smashed a bottle of champagne on the other engine's tender. It was all very touching. And it wasn't so long ago, either.

Once it had made a good start, railway development progressed faster in America than in any other country. It became a mania. Railroads sprang up everywhere. Many of them were used for years for stock manipulation but more of them really opened up new fields. They were so numerous for a time, however, that it was often necessary to buy a dozen tickets to get from one city to another, and to use as many roads.

They were a bit slow in becoming luxurious and the early travelers weren't exactly comfortable. However, late in the '50s Mr. George Pullman, who started as a cabinet maker and later became a successful Chicago contractor, developed the sleeping car. The first one of these was nothing about which to get excited. It was lighted by candles and heated by two small stoves at the ends. It had four berths which were not so soft as they might have been. But Mr. Pullman worked on the idea and eventually did well with it.

In 1867, on the Grand Trunk Railroad, Mr. Pullman turned one of his sleeping cars into a "hotel car." He set up a small kitchen at one end and placed tables in the room that remained. And his men served broiled beefsteak and potatoes for sixty cents, broiled ham for fifty, lobster salad for forty, and an omelet with pre-Volstead rum for thirty-five.

Part of the development of railroads lay in the field of speed, too. The early engines did very well in this regard. The first engine built in America was capable of twenty-one miles an hour. But this was only under perfect conditions and without carrying a load. The great advance in the field of speed came with the development of safety appliances. When men had found ways to keep trains on their tracks most of the time they worked out the problem of giving them more power.

In the '40s trains had become so rapid that the word "express" was used to classify those that made direct and rapid runs between fairly distant points with speed as their object. The term "express" came from a package-delivery service originated by William Frederick Harnden, a railway conductor, and first tried between New York and Boston.

"Lightning express" was devised, probably, by a smart advertising man. Trains never have achieved the speed of lightning. We of another era, who are beginning to think of railroads as just a shade old-fashioned, know better than that. Even airplanes can't go that fast!

BEFORE BABE RUTH

Chapter XVII: Before Babe Ruth

BASEBALL has not always been America's national game. The general interest in the pastime is of comparatively recent origin. But then, for that matter, in a country the civilization of which is only a couple of centuries old almost everything is of comparatively recent origin.

The earliest of our settlers were not what might be called playful. Most of them had come here with their heads full of the sort of religion that frowned on pleasure. The Puritans considered it, if not sinful, at least frivolous to indulge in games.

Not only that, but they had a great many other things to which to turn their attention. Digging into a new country and making it a paying proposition meant work. They had little leisure. Then, too, the Indians had a way of annoying them. The fear of the pesky, as the saying goes, redskins was constantly with them and did not make for relaxation.

However, the Dutch, who moved into New York, were naturally a gay people. They came to America to make money and had no problems of theology to worry them. They went to church, when they had a church, and that was that. They had less to fear from the Indians than the others because they knew better how to deal with them. And so they had more time to play.

Most of their games were simple. They played backgammon in their taverns and they bowled on their greens. Others of their pastimes were not quite so pretty. For instance, there was the one called "clubbing the cat." For this a rope was stretched between two iron spikes and a loosely cooped barrel suspended in its center. A live cat was placed in the barrel. The players withdrew an agreed distance and hurled heavy clubs at the barrel. The one who freed the cat won the game. Frequently he also killed the cat.

Then there was "pulling the goose." For this a goose with its head greased was tied lightly to a rope anchored to a peg at the side of the road. Contestants rode past on horses, leaning over and trying to grasp the goose. The man who carried it off won. His prize was the goose, which was the basis of an excellent Dutch dinner. More often than not it wasn't necessary to kill the bird for the cooking. The game had seen to that.

The Dutch had various ball games, too, played with a lopsided sphere stuffed with horsehair. Eventually these became a sort of baseball. It was played in New England as well as New York. There were "throwers" and there were "batters." There was no limit to those who could play. On town-meeting day as many as forty would participate. There were casualties, too, for to retire a base runner in those days it was necessary to hit him personally with a thrown ball.

The game continued to thrive in odd forms until a Mr. Abner Doubleday of Cooperstown, N. Y., took it in hand in 1839. He set down its rules, limited its players to nine on each side, and held that it must be played upon a diamond-shaped field. Six years later the first real baseball team was formed and a national pastime was in the making.

This first baseball team, the Knickerbockers, of New York, had no chance to test its ability because it was the only team in the country. Its members repaired regularly to Hoboken, N. J., across the river, where they prepared to meet a non-existent foe. Finally, in 1846, another team was organized, taking the name New Yorks, and issued a challenge.

And so the first baseball game on record was played in Hoboken on June 19, 1846. The stake was a dinner for all concerned and the challengers won 23 to 1. They required only four innings, the rules then specifying that the game ended in the inning in which one team reached a total of twenty-one runs.

Evidently the New Yorks could not stand prosperity for they seem to have disbanded with their victory. The Knickerbockers, therefore, had to wait five years for another game. By this time they had adopted uniforms consisting of blue trousers, white shirts, and, of all things, straw hats. The Washington club, of Yorkville, challenged them in 1851 and lost 21 to 11 in eight innings.

In the next few years the game began to take hold and nines sprang up in various parts of the East. And at this point the Knickerbockers all but prevented the pastime from becoming national. They were the aristocrats of the sport and they resented the fact that uncouth boilermakers and shipwrights were taking up the diamond. They refused to accept any challenges and played only among themselves.

The game had reached the stage at which it needed organization. The rules wanted revision. Nothing could be done without the recognized champions. And the champions would do nothing but hold banquets. Finally, in 1857, the Knickerbockers were flattered into calling a convention. Twenty-five clubs sent representatives. The champions were permitted to run the proceedings that year but the following year another meeting was held and they didn't stand a chance. They were out-voted on every suggestion and did not even elect an officer.

From that moment baseball became a democratic game. The Civil War served to popularize it still further. The soldiers used their time between battles for baseball games. It is even reported that during the siege of Richmond the rival armies had so little to do that they declared a brief truce and sent a Blue team against a Gray one. The Confederates, running true to form, are reported to have lost. When the soldiers went back to their homes they took baseball with them and soon every city of any size had its nine.

The game, however, still was on an amateur footing. The only gate money that had ever been charged up to 1869 was for a game between New York and Brooklyn clubs. It was found that considerable expense had been incurred in preparing a field for the tilt. To raise funds for this spectators were charged a fee of fifty cents. Fifteen hundred of them paid it.

In 1869, however, the Cincinnati Red Stockings defied convention and announced that they would pay their players regular salaries. They proceeded to get together a brilliant team, which trouped the country and won eighty-one games without a single defeat. The experiment was so successful that other cities followed suit. Leagues eventually were formed and now baseball is a major industry, with at least one player who receives more each year than the President of the United States.

THE AMERICAN NATIONAL GAME OF BASE BALL.

GRAND MATCH FOR THE CHAMPIONSHIP AT THE ELYSIAN FIELDS, HOBOKEN, N. J.

PAINTED BY JOHN TRUMBULL.

LITHOGRAPHED BY N. CURRIER, N.Y.

ENTERED ACCORDING TO ACT OF CONGRESS IN THE YEAR 1852 BY N. CURRIER, IN THE CLERKS OFFICE OF THE DISTRICT COURT OF THE SOUTHERN DISTRICT OF N.Y.

SURRENDER OF GENERAL BURGOYNE AT SARATOGA N.Y. OCT 17TH 1777.

AND HOWE!

Chapter XVIII: And Howe!

WARS are not won on the battlefield, according to a timeless theory, advanced, quite probably, by the first non-combatant. If the reasoning be sound it is safe to assume that neither are they lost there. Americans need not go beyond their own Revolution to prove the point.

Tacticians have said that Mr. John Burgoyne let the American Colonies slip through his king's fingers when he surrendered his buffeted redcoats at Saratoga. There is no quarrel with the statement that the Battle of Saratoga was the turning point of the Revolution. But it was lost by a stupid little man in London, miles away. It was lost almost a year before it was fought. John Burgoyne was little to blame. However, he must be the central figure in his own story and he had deficiencies enough for that.

He was born, this "Gentleman Johnny," in London in 1722. The records say he was the son of Sir John Burgoyne, but it was whispered about before he was well swaddled that he was the illegitimate issue of Lord Bingley. Not whispered exactly, either, for the affronted Lady Bingley fairly shouted it. Legitimate or not, he grew to be a handsome devil and more than a bit of a swashbuckler. When he came to marry he chose to elope, taking for his runaway bride Lady Charlotte

Stanley, who was, statistically, the sixth daughter of the eleventh Earl of Derby.

He was, at the time, an officer in the First Dragoons and far too fond of cards. The cards, however, were not reciprocally affectionate, and in 1747 he was forced to sell his commission to pay his debts. He settled in France for a time but, by 1756, was back in uniform, thanks to the influence of his father-in-law. He saw service in the Seven Years' War, helped introduce light cavalry into the British army, and participated in the clash with Spain over Portugal. He sat in Parliament long enough to make a few speeches too flowery to mean anything. And he wrote a play or two.

His literary pretensions, in fact, made him something of a bore. When he was sent to America to help subdue the rebels in the vicinity of Boston he devoted most of his time to the composition of high-sounding letters.

To his superiors in England he wrote that he believed he could bring the recalcitrants to a better frame of mind if he were given permission to go afield as a diplomatist. When George Washington protested the treatment of captured American officers, General Burgoyne replied by giving him advice as to how to run a revolution in a dignified manner. He almost got into trouble too, when, in a letter to General Charles Lee, of the American forces, he presumed to set forth the conditions under which the British would talk peace.

Eventually he was called home and, on occasions when he rode with King George in Hyde Park, found an opportunity to present his scheme for a campaign to be waged from Canada, the purpose of which was to split the Colonies in half with a redcoat line and thus end the American annoyance.

As a matter of tactical fact, it was an excellent plan, and might well have eliminated the possibility of any United States of America. Burgoyne was to drive down from Canada and Howe was to march up from Albany. When they met the rebel forces would be hopelessly cut off from each other and the insurrection would be over. It all looked very simple there in London and Burgoyne set sail for Quebec.

But wars are not won and lost on the battlefield. Lord George Germain had promised to send General Howe a full account of the proposed procedure "on the first packet." The instructions were prepared but, on the day on which they were to be signed, Lord George was in a hurry to be off to Kent on a holiday and, being impatient as well as stupid, couldn't wait to sign them. He quite forgot about them when he got back and they never went forth.

Burgoyne reached Canada early in 1777 and set off with an army of 8,000, half of whom were Germans, Canadians, and Indians, to do his share of the job. He had no difficulty in frightening a half-starved and unrelieved garrison out of Ticonderoga, and then he started through the treacherous woods for Saratoga.

On the way he paused to replenish his supply of mounts and food. An unintelligent intelligence officer suggested a raid on Bennington, Vt., and Burgoyne sent a detachment of Germans on the errand. They encountered a belligerent band of rebels. The captain of the troops sent to relieve them was not on speaking terms with the German commander and took his time for spite. The result was a severe loss of men and morale but Burgoyne pushed on.

Meantime, however, Howe was not moving north. He was, in fact, doing just the opposite. Having at the moment no lady to dandle on his knee (the general was a great one for the ladies and lost more than one skirmish because of them) he thought it would be amusing to capture Philadelphia. And so he did.

Therefore, when General Burgoyne reached the plains of Saratoga and the camp of the American army, under General Horatio Gates, he had only a gambler's chance. He could have retreated. But there was a possibility that he could break through. He was a gambler. He attacked. At first there was success. Then the tide began to turn. General Burgoyne found himself hemmed in on all sides and no help in sight.

It is reported by an eavesdropper that on the night before his disaster General Burgoyne drank a great deal of champagne and shared a tent with the wife of a commissary. It may very well be true. It was what a gambler might have done. His soldiery had failed him. He was handsome and he knew at least one field in which he could win.

Next morning he called his staff together and outlined the situation. It was too late now to turn back. He asked whether they believed he could surrender honorably. They said they did. So he dispatched a messenger to General Gates and, after considerable negotiation, articles of convention, worthy of a Twentieth Century naval conference, were drawn up and signed.

On the morning of October 10th, General Burgoyne "in a rich royal uniform" rode to the enemy's camp, doffed his hat, and said:

"The fortune of war, General Gates, has made me your prisoner."

And the little man in London who had been in such a hurry to get to Kent was pretty angry when he heard about it.

THE END